The
of Power

The Gender of Power

KATHY DAVIS
MONIQUE LEIJENAAR
JANTINE OLDERSMA

SAGE Publications
London • Newbury Park • New Delhi

Editorial arrangement and selection © Kathy Davis,
Monique Leijenaar and Jantine Oldersma 1991
Introduction © Jantine Oldersma and Kathy Davis 1991
Chapter 1 © Joan Meyer 1991
Chapter 2 © Aafke Komter 1991
Chapter 3 © Kathy Davis 1991
Chapter 4 © Joan Wolffensperger 1991
Chapter 5 © Annelies Moors 1991
Chapter 6 © Riet Delsing 1991
Chapter 7 © Carla Risseeuw 1991

First published 1991

 SAGE Publications Ltd
6 Bonhill Street
London EC2A 4PU

SAGE Publications Inc
2455 Teller Road
Newbury Park, California 91320

SAGE Publications India Pvt Ltd
32, M-Block Market
Greater Kailash – I
New Delhi 110 048

British Library Cataloguing in Publication data

The gender of power.
  I. Davis, Kathy   II. Leijenaar, Monique
  III. Oldersma, Jantine
  305.3

ISBN 0-8039-8542-8
ISBN 0-8039-8543-6 pbk

Library of Congress catalog card number 91-53088

Typeset by AKM Associates (UK) Ltd, Southall, London
Printed in Great Britain by J.W. Arrowsmith Ltd, Bristol

Contents

Preface

In this volume, the subject of the 'battle of the sexes', which
has enjoyed such popularity in the fine arts throughout the
ages, will be given some scholarly attention. The relationship between gender and power has always been a central
concern of feminist scholarship. It has not proved an easy
relationship to come to terms with, however. The conceptualization of both gender and power, as well as how they
are related, often gives rise to more questions than
answers. For example, are gender relations so specific that
a specific theory on gender is required in order to explain
them? And, if this is so, what are those special features
which distinguish gender relations from other relations of
power between dominant and subordinate groups? Given
that relations between men and women are integrally
connected with power, perhaps they may best be tackled
within the already long and venerable tradition of theories
on power. After all, if social theory can provide promising
insights on power, should we not be able to put it to use for
our own feminist ends? Would it not be possible to adapt
existing power theories to the special features of gender
relations, perhaps after some critical feminist deconstruc-
tion? Or, should we be devoting our energies toward
developing our own theories of power? What if the
mainstream power theories themselves are so irrevocably
gendered that only a feminist perspective on power will
do? We feel that questions like these are at the heart of the
newly emerging discipline of women's studies. Not only do
they touch on the *raison d'être* of the field, but they raise the

problem of the relationship between feminist theory and social theory, traditional and critical alike.

These questions will be addressed in the essays in this volume. The essays were originally written for a symposium, 'The Gender of Power', held at the University of Leiden in the winter of 1987. They provide an overview of the various ways in which the relationship between gender and power is tackled by Dutch feminist scholars. They attempt to clarify some of the conceptual problems inherent in the relationship between gender and power while, at the same time, remaining firmly grounded in the study of gender relations in various contexts of everyday life.

The authors in this volume come from different disciplines and theoretical perspectives and have approached the conceptualization of power and gender in a variety of ways, depending on the practical and theoretical problems encountered in the course of their own particular inquiries. It is our hope that we will not only generate debate among other feminist scholars about the necessity of dealing more explicitly with power in our theories on gender, but that we will have provided some useful guidelines for women's studies research on gender relations as well.

Finally, a few words of thanks are in order. We are indebted to Els Postel-Coster and Joyce Outshoorn for becoming the first professors of women's studies at the University of Leiden, thereby providing us with an excuse for this project. Dini Vos put countless hours into organizing the conference upon which this book is based and, generally, helping to get things started. Lutgart Delvaux provided support and encouragement midway through the project. Special thanks go to Rosemary Gunn for preliminary editing and to Nelly Steffens for the final product. And, finally, we would like to express our appreciation to Karen Phillips, who never stopped believing that we would have the power to finish this book.

About the Authors

Kathy Davis is an associate professor of women's studies in the Faculty of Social Sciences at the University of Utrecht in The Netherlands. She received a degree in clinical psychology at the Free University in Amsterdam and has taught women's studies and psychology at various universities in The Netherlands. Her research interests and publications focus on gender and power in professional caretaking, feminist theory, discourse analysis and rhetoric.

Riet Delsing studied cultural anthropology at the University of Leiden. She worked in Chile on a number of projects concerning human rights and women's issues between 1973 and 1985. Back in Holland in 1987 she did a Master's Degree in Women and Development at the Institute of Social Studies in the Hague. She is currently living in Santiago and involved in research, consultancy work on women's issues and publishing women's books.

Aafke Komter studied psychology at the University of Amsterdam and was a C. and C. Huijgens scholar at the Institute of Sociology at the University of Leiden. She has published extensively on marital relations and power and is now engaged in research on power, responsibility and gender relations in the field of paid labor. Recent publications are on the 'dilemma' of difference and equality, the responsible society and Hannah Arendt's concept of power. She is currently employed at the Department of General Social Sciences of the University of Utrecht.

Monique Leijenaar is an associate professor in the Department of Political Science of the University of Nijmegen. She has published extensively on electoral behavior and the political representation of women. She is a member of the editorial board of *Women and Politics*.

Joan Meyer is currently employed at the Department of Organizational Psychology of the University of Amsterdam, where she teaches and carries out research on organizational culture, planned change in organizations and conflict resolution. Her PhD thesis, 'Gender as an Organizational Principle' (1983), dealt with unequal power relations between women and men.

Annelies Moors is an anthropologist. She works at the Research and Documentation Center Women and Autonomy of the University of Leiden as well as the University of Amsterdam. She is currently engaged in historical and anthropological research on gender, production and property on the West Bank.

Jantine Oldersma studied political science and works at the Department of Women's Studies of the University of Leiden. She has published articles on gender and popular literature, including romantic novels and detective fiction in numerous feminist journals. She is currently engaged in research on women in the Dutch political elite.

Carla Risseeuw is an anthropologist, currently working as a senior researcher at the Third World Center of the University of Nijmegen. She has regularly published as well as directed films on topics related to women in Sri Lanka and has been involved in a Sri Lankan organization of home-based women workers for the past 13 years. At present she is engaged in research in Kenya on changing gender and kinship relations, as a follow-up of research of 17 years ago.

Joan Wolffensperger studied sociology of Third World countries at the University of Wageningen and worked as a consultant and researcher in Surinam. She is now a teacher and researcher in the field of women's studies at the University of Wageningen and is currently working on a dissertation on feminist principles in the practice of university education.

Introduction

JANTINE OLDERSMA AND KATHY DAVIS

Within feminist scholarship, the notion that there is a connection between gender and power is a familiar one. Gender inequality is, after all, a pervasive feature in much of social life. It is the familiar thread that not only meanders through most of our everyday practices, but crosses national boundaries and moves backward and forward through time. Despite the variety of forms gender inequality takes and has taken in the past, it remains something that can be perceived in various otherwise highly dissimilar settings and cultures.

The relationship between gender and power has been treated as a given within feminist scholarship of the past two decades. The precise nature of this relationship, however, remains shadowy. Despite the centrality of both concepts for feminists, constructing theories which can satisfactorily account for how they are connected has proved particularly troublesome.

In this volume, we have collected together essays dealing with the ways in which theories of power might be applied to gender relations or, to be more precise, with how gender relations can be conceptualized as power relations in the first place. Before embarking on a more detailed examination of some of the issues raised by the authors in this volume concerning the study of power relations between the sexes, a brief historical sketch may be helpful to put the relationship between power and gender into perspective.

Feminist scholarship and gender

> It is opportune, perhaps today even mandatory, that
> we develop a more relevant psychology and philosophy
> of power relationships beyond the simple conceptual
> framework provided by our traditional formal politics.
> Indeed, it may be imperative that we give some
> attention to defining a theory of politics which treats
> power relationships on grounds less conventional than
> those to which we are accustomed. (Millett 1969: 24)

This plea for a more inclusive theory of power was made by
Kate Millett in 1969 and with it came her pioneering
introduction of the notion of 'sexual politics'. The second
wave of the feminist movement was already in full swing in
the worldwide context of women's growing dissatisfaction
with their subordinate social position. Sexual differences
were no longer accepted as natural or biological and,
consequently, part of the god-given order of things.
Instead, they were viewed as the result of relations
involving domination and subordination. 'Sexual politics'
provided the conceptual banner under which relations
between the sexes could be defined as a political issue and
feminists could unite, entering the political arena thus
defined to do battle against female subordination in all
walks of social life.

   In the wake of the second wave, feminist scholars began
to make their laborious way into academia, struggling to
get their concerns included in the university curriculum
and research programs. 'Sexual politics' was at the top of
the agenda for most of these early scholars as well. Their
interest arose, in part, as a result of their own position as
underpaid and under-represented members of the academic
community and as a response to the androcentric biases
which they were discovering within their own disciplines.
As feminists, however, they were also committed to
explaining how and why relations between the sexes came

to involve male domination and female subordination and, more to the point, how this unfortunate state of affairs might be altered.

Before feminist scholars could get on with this task, they found themselves having to deal with an all-too-familiar stumbling block. First, gender inequality had to be established for the non-believers as a problem: something that existed and, therefore, could be studied. Just as their activist sisters were faced with having to establish that women were a political group, sharing common problems, interests, and a (more or less) common view of how to ameliorate them (de Vries 1987), academic women had to establish their concerns as topics, meriting scientific attention within the hallowed halls of science. Thus, before investigating how asymmetrical gender relations were being produced and reproduced in the context of women's everyday lives, early feminists had first to convince the predominantly male gatekeepers of academic resources that there was, indeed, something to study.

Since the (male) academic community had historically displayed the tendency to treat relations between the sexes as part of the 'natural order', that is, as normal and, therefore, intrinsically unproblematic, the umbilical cord between biology and asymmetries in relations between the sexes had to be severed, (as was optimistically hoped) once and for all. To this end, the sex/gender distinction was formulated (Oakley 1972).

Drawing upon evidence provided by transsexuals or persons whose biological sex was open to dispute, Oakley demonstrated that sexual identity was not determined strictly by anatomy, but was primarily a social and cultural construction. The relativity of biological sex was further underlined by anthropological findings on gender distinctions. They showed that differences between the sexes existed in every culture. However, gender identity not only varied greatly from one culture to the next, but the forms it took tended to be contradictory as well (Chodorow 1971;

Rosaldo and Lamphere 1974). For example, the feminine ideal in one culture might be physical strength and material self-sufficiency, whereas in another, femininity resided precisely in women's proclivity toward weakness and dependency. It became clear that sexual difference was not the biological bedrock it had been cracked up to be. It seemed instead to be little more than an arbitrary hodge-podge of social and cultural constructions.

By introducing gender as a theoretical construct, it became possible for the first time to transfer relations between the sexes from biology to society. At the same time, the locus of sexual asymmetries shifted from nature to social relations. If it was not woman's anatomical destiny to be weak, victimized and poor, then the culprit had to be sought elsewhere. By establishing sexual difference as a social or cultural product, the path was opened toward locating relations between the sexes with other socially structured relations of power. The subordination of women could no longer be explained (away) by her biology, but had entered the realm of the social and, more to the point, the political: as power relations, gender asymmetries were socially produced and reproduced and, therefore, subject to transformation. In short, gender as a theoretical construct was instrumental in the emergence of feminist scholarship. It enabled feminists to establish a whole range of issues which had previously been unthinkable, let alone meriting serious scholarly attention.

The concept of gender

The concept of gender has since moved from its original function in establishing the distinction between biology and society to the position of undisputed central theoretical construct within the field of feminist scholarship. A substantial portion of feminist theory construction has gone into developing theories of gender, elaborating gender as the 'fundamental organizing principle' for explaining divisions in women's and men's experiences (Rubin 1975; Coward 1983a; Harding and Hintikka 1983; Hartsock 1983; Harding 1986; Scott 1986, 1988; de Lauretis 1987). Gender is central for understanding sexual dichotomies, behavioral differences between the sexes, sexual identity, sexual divisions in social activities and the symbolic representation of masculinity and femininity (Hagemann-White 1989).

These developments in feminist theory have certainly broadened our understanding of sexual difference as a many-splendored phenomenon, sporting multiple layers of meaning and numerous levels of abstraction. Ironically, however, the very complexity and multiplicity of the phenomenon set limits on the use of gender as theoretical category. In particular, as soon as we turn to our original problem of what makes gender relations hierarchically structured, we begin to run into trouble.

To begin with, gender is a descriptive rather than an explanatory concept. As such, it is, and continues to be, useful for uncovering differences in male and female experiences, social positions, behavior or whatever. It provides a way of pinpointing potential problem areas and showing where further study is required. Gender differences, in and of themselves, however, do not indicate why relations between women and men so regularly seem to involve domination and subordination. Nor does gender account for the dynamics of these relations; how they come to be produced, reproduced and transformed in the various contexts of everyday life. Abandoning the automatic link between gender and power may have been instrumental for women's studies in order to gain respectability as a new discipline. However, it also threatens to take the sting out of a feminist critique of power asymmetries in relations between the sexes (Outshoorn 1989). Recent attempts to reconnect power and gender by redefining gender as a 'primary way of signifying relationships of power' (Scott

1986: 1069) as well as difference are a step in the right direction. However, they mark what should be the beginning of an empirical and theoretical investigation into gender relations rather than its conclusion. We are still left with the task of having to proceed from gender differences to power and it is precisely this relationship which remains cloudy and inadequately conceptualized within feminist scholarship (Davis 1988b).

A second and more serious problem with gender as a theoretical construct is that it seems to imply that relations between the sexes are in some way specific or different from other relations between subordinate and dominant groups. This specificity has been situated in various areas: in women's social position as the providers of domestic services, both on a paid and unpaid basis (Hartmann 1979a), in women's reproductive capacity (O'Brien 1981) or in female sexuality (Hartsock 1983). Unfortunately, relations involving domination and subordination tend to be unequal in more than one way. Power is conflated (Davis 1988b), making it difficult to sort out what is happening as a result of gendered structures and what needs to be attributed to the social class, ethnic background or nationality of the participants. When we investigate gender relations in daily life, we generally discover that all of these structured forms of domination are 'continually being redefined in the process of ongoing political and ideological struggles; they are never static' (Fee 1986: 53). Asymmetrical power relations rarely allow themselves to be tidily taken apart and given a single source of causality, be it gender or some other form of hierarchy.

In short, gender may have accomplished what it set out to do; namely, establishing relations between the sexes as a problem requiring further investigation. However, it may not be the most useful concept for investigating what makes these relations asymmetrical or how these asymmetries are produced, reproduced and transformed in social life.

Social theory of power

The difficulties inherent in the gender concept may account for recent trends in feminist scholarship to take another look at the problem of power. If theories of gender do not lead us unproblematically to our goal of uncovering and explaining the various faces and forms of male domination and female subordination, what about power? After all, power as a theoretical construct does tend to take asymmetrical relations and the ways that they are produced, reproduced and transformed as its object. Unlike gender, however, power is not a new concept, but has a long history behind it. We could even say that the notion of power is as old as (social) science itself, and certainly one of the mainstays of scientific debate since the turn of the century.

Take, for example, Weber's celebrated definition of power which served as a starting point for social theories on power. Power is 'the chance of a man or of a number of men to realize their own will in a communal action even against the resistance of others' (Weber 1978: 926). Similar conceptions of power can be found in theorists as diverse as Hobbes and, more recently, Russell and the early writings of Dahl (Davis 1988b). According to this definition, if A can make B do something which B would not be likely to do when left to his/her own devices, power has been exercised. Power is linked to the purposive action of individuals. Exercising power seems to be inherently asymmetrical.

Simple as this conception of power seemed, it immediately raised a host of serious problems. For example, if power is inevitably tied to action or intention, how are we to explain the situation which emerges when A manages to convince B that he or she wants to do A's bidding? Does this mean that power has not been exercised? Or, must we include more covert, semi-intentional forms in our arsenal of power plays? Another problem is presented by those unfortunate situations where the opportunities for action and, therefore, the exercise of power, are unequally distributed before the interaction begins. Can we talk about power being exercised in this case and, if so, where are the culprits? If the asymmetrical distribution of opportunities for exercising power is not a matter of chance but rather a feature of social structures, what kinds of consequences does this have for how we view an individual's ability to exercise control over his/her own fate?

These difficulties resulted in a move away from power as the intentional activity of individuals toward theories which treated power as a structural property of collectivities or communities. Take, for example, another illustrious social theorist, Parsons, who defined power as: 'a generalized capacity to serve the performance of binding obligations by units in a system of collective organization when the obligations are legitimized with reference to their bearing on collective goals' (Parsons 1963: 237). Durkheim, Marx, Arendt and, more recently, Poulantzas are all proponents of the view that power is a structural feature of society. Power is the medium by which collective interests may be realized, including class interests. Whether these interests were shared by all members of society was itself a matter of debate, with Parsons and Ahrendt emphasizing the consensual aspects of power, and Marx and Poulantzas focusing on conflict. However, these theorists were in agreement that theories of power needed to take into account that people act under conditions which are not of their own choosing and which they only partially oversee (Davis 1988b).

Although structural perspectives on power alleviated some of the difficulties inherent in the Weberian conception of power, they did not, by any means, provide the final word on the problem of power. For example, if power is a structural feature of society, where do these structures come from and how are they maintained? What is the connection between structures of power and the everyday social practices of individuals and groups? And, most important of all, how are we to account for transformations in asymmetrical power relations? In short, if power is 'out there' in the social order, how do we go about finding it?

In recent years, theorists like Lukes, Wrong, Connolly, Giddens, Bourdieu, Elias and, of course, Foucault have also turned to the age-old problem of power. Drawing upon a diversity of theoretical traditions, an attempt was made to come up with more sophisticated answers to the question of what power is and how it can be delineated in the various contexts of social life (Gremmen and Westerbeek-van Eerten 1988). New kinds of issues emerged in the debate on power. For example, the notion that conflict, whether between individuals or groups, was a convenient starting point for the analysis of power was abandoned for a less-simplified approach. It was argued that power was also involved in situations where no overt conflict was present. Indeed, it was part of the very fabric of the system, taking the form of a 'mobilization of bias' which prevented the outbreak of conflict. In many cases, opposition remains unarticulated and even scarcely perceived by the parties themselves (Bachrach and Baratz 1970; Lukes 1974).

Another conceptual problem concerned the relationship between the individual power practices of Weber and the structured forms of power as described by Parsons et al. Whereas earlier theorists tended to treat power dualistically, as the intentional practices of individuals or as a structural feature of social systems and collectivities, contemporary power theories seem to want a reconciliation. Whereas no self-respecting critical social scientist was prepared to deny power a structural base, the relationship between actors and their social practices to the constitution of society began to be seen as an essential ingredient for understanding the workings of power. This led to the development of sophisticated conceptual frameworks for linking agency and structure (Bourdieu 1977; Giddens 1979).

The relationship between historical change and subjectivity also posed problems for modern theorists of power. Confronted with long-term processes of social transformation, it became clear that shifts in the balance of power cannot be foreseen, let alone intended, by the participants. Conceptions of power were needed which could deal with structural changes operating outside the activities and consciousness of individuals. This required, however, new ways of thinking about subjectivity and the nature of agency. Some theorists, like Foucault, declared the subject to be defunct, a mere linguistic creation. History was made 'without a subject' and power became part and parcel of the micro-processes of social life (Foucault 1983). Others like Bourdieu (1977), Elias (1972) and Giddens (1979, 1984) called for a reconceptualization of agency which could link individual activities and broader social processes. The focus shifted to the routine, habitual and practical features of human conduct in the constitution of social life. In this way, the reproduction and transformation of social structures in patterned ways could be accounted for without having to rely on the intentions of individuals or groups as explanation.

These developments made it possible to look for power in hitherto unlikely places: in cultural discourses, in the ordinary workings of everyday life, in intimate and even friendly relations. Whereas power had previously been linked to the public sphere of political parties, social movements or institutions, it now became much more ubiquitous. At the same time, the analysis of power became a matter of exploring boundaries, breaks and discontinuities, rather than straightforwardly accounting for the material division of goods and opportunities. The new power theorists were clearly more willing to embrace power in all its contradictory and multifaceted diversity than their predecessors had been. Power became accepted as one of the 'essentially contested concepts' (Lukes 1974) of the social sciences.

Taken together, these developments in social theories on power paved the way for the feminist entry into the field. Just as feminists were discovering that power needed to be dealt with more explicitly in their accounts of gender relations and that gender theory needed to include a perspective on power, they encountered a debate on power within the social sciences which looked as if it might have something to offer. Feminist scholars are old-hands at taking conceptual frameworks apart and subjecting them to critical scrutiny. The activities of redefining and reformulating have always belonged to feminist inquiry. Moreover, most feminists would be the first to admit that the traditional concepts of the social sciences are contested and that solutions to theoretical problems are frequently of a tentative and temporary type. Thus, it is not surprising that feminist scholars began to overcome some of their original mistrust of the (male) mainstream, returning, hesitantly to be sure, and with critical faculties well intact, to social theories on power to see what they had to offer for understanding asymmetrical relations between the sexes (Gremmen and Westerbeek-van Eerten 1988).

Gender and power

Despite the growing complexity and sophistication of contemporary power theory, it proved insufficient when it came to dealing with power in practice. Theorists displayed a certain reticence when it came to the mundane task of applying their theories to the study of power in the social contexts of everyday life. Moreover, many were reluctant to include gender as a relevant feature of power. Within feminist scholarship, there have been several notable attempts to link gender and power. For example, Hartsock (1983) attempts to develop a specifically feminist perspective on power.

She begins with a comprehensive critique of traditional

theories of power in political philosophy (Blau, Talcott Parsons, Dahl) as well as more recent power theories in critical social science (Bachrach and Baratz, Lukes). Her analysis shows how they are all based on a contract model of power (power relations as competitive encounters between self-interested, autonomous individuals). She confronts this model with several female theories of power (Arendt, Emmett) which stress the communal aspects of power or the ability 'to act in concert'. In this way, she can make a case for the 'gendered-ness' of power theories; that is, the location of the theorist will affect what he/she sees when it comes to delineating power. Hartsock argues, however, that a 'feminine' view of power needs to be expanded with a historical materialist analysis of relations of domination and subordination between the sexes to provide a truly feminist perspective on power and gender.

Another attempt to connect power and gender is provided by Connell (1987). He takes early feminist theory on asymmetrical relations between the sexes as a starting point. According to Connell, feminist theory was on the right track in pinpointing the various inequities in gender relations. However, it has tended to fall short due to an inadequate conceptualization of gender. Gender was either tied to an inadequate sex-roles framework (which Connell proceeds thoroughly to dismantle) or embedded in Marxist frameworks which left little conceptual space for the active and knowledgeable 'actress'. He concludes with a practice-oriented conception of gendered power, reminiscent of the work of Bourdieu and Giddens, which can combat the ills of dualistic notions of power and gender.

In addition to these theoretical attempts to come to terms with the relationship between power and gender, numerous feminist scholars in various disciplines have explored the actual workings of power, showing how asymmetrical gender relations are produced and reproduced in concrete social contexts. It is hardly possible to open a book on gender relations without power being an essential, if implicit, part of the story. However, there have been few attempts to weave power theories and empirical work on gender relations together. This would require, on the one hand, a careful look at some of the potentialities and pitfalls of various theories on power for investigating gender relations. On the other hand, this appraisal would need to be grounded in the specific contexts and particular problems of the inquiry in question.

It is precisely these missing links which will be the focus of the present volume. The central problem concerns how existing power theories and gender are to be connected in feminist research on relations between the sexes. Each of the authors has taken (critical) social theory on power as her starting point. Lukes (1974, 1986), Giddens (1979, 1984), Bourdieu (1977), Foucault (1980), as well as the materialist tradition within the social sciences, are critically evaluated in terms of their usefulness for understanding gender relations. Both the possibilities and problems offered by the various theoretical frameworks for doing research on gendered contexts are explored.

The volume is organized into three sections. Each deals with ways that power theory would need to be elaborated in order to account for the complexities of gender relations. In the first part, the necessity of extending conceptions of power to include covert, consensual or even intimate relations is tackled. Lukes' theory of power as three-dimensional is drawn upon for help in this particular project.

Joan Meyer makes use of the work of Lukes in order to understand power in intimate relations between men and women. Since the majority of women are blessed with fathers, brothers, sons, lovers and/or husbands – relationships which form a central and integral part of their lives – it is impossible to uncover the workings of power unless our theoretical notions of power include conceptual space for love. It is this specific intertwining of power and love in gender relations which makes power gendered.

Aafke Komter shows how a conception of power which draws upon insights from Lukes and Gramsci can be helpful in uncovering the hidden face of power in marital relations. She argues that there is not one kind of power. Unlike Meyer, she suggests that the mechanisms, socio-cultural manifestations and social consequences of power operate in a similar fashion for all asymmetrical social relations. Gender relations are, however, typical for situations where power operates through ideological hegemony.

In the second part, the relationship between the practices of individuals and social structures of domination and subordination is discussed. Giddens' theory of structuration is the starting point for the authors in this section.

Kathy Davis criticizes the tendency in feminist theory toward using top-down, repressive models of power to understand asymmetrical gender relations. The argument is put forth that theories of power are needed which can retrieve women as basically competent social actors as well as providing a more nuanced version of how power works in relations between the sexes. She shows how current discussions on power in social theory and, in particular, Giddens' conception of power are of use in ensuring that women do not become 'cultural dopes' in feminist studies of gender relations.

Joan Wolffensperger also draws upon Giddens' structuration theory to shed light on gender and power. Taking hierarchies in university education as a case in point, she criticizes traditional explanations which have looked to the psychological make-up of individual women or their heavy responsibilities for the care of husbands and children to understand segregation according to sex. By viewing the university as system, subtle 'gendered structures' may be uncovered which account for the reproduction of gender differences in education. Giddens' theory enables her to bridge the gap between the behavior of individual men and women and the structural properties of social systems such as universities and schools. In this way, both 'victim-blaming' and deterministic explanations can be avoided.

In the third section, sites of power practices for women, both as individuals and collectives, are discussed. In particular, the interconnection of subjectivity and historical change is explored. To this end, theories of Foucault, Bourdieu, Goody and Tambiah are drawn upon.

In a research project conducted among women on the Palestinian West Bank, Annelies Moors explores shifts in relations of power between the sexes. Whereas theorists like Goody and Tambiah, operating in the materialist tradition of anthropology, tend to treat property as a relatively uncomplicated resource of power, Moors shows that gender constrains how property is employed and what it means for the power of the property-holder. Historical transformations cannot be explained without taking cultural representations of gender and gender inequality as constitutive for power relations into account.

Riet Delsing draws upon Foucault's work on sovereign and disciplinary forms of power in order to understand the contradictions in women's political participation in post-Allende Chile. Organization is frequently seen as a source of power, crucial to women's (lack of) influence in politics. In organizing for a democratic society, Chilean women had to wage battle on two fronts: against the regime and against their male comrades. Delsing attributes the failure of the women's movement in Chile to maintain its momentum for any length of time to its inability to distinguish the more subtle disciplinary power practices of individual men from the sovereign power of the government. This resulted in their tendency to overemphasize political rights and neglect power practices of the more mundane variety, where women continually constitute their identities as political subjects.

The apparent failure of women to apprehend changes in their social position is also the starting point of Carla Risseeuw's chapter on the historical transformation of gender relations in Sri Lanka under colonial rule. The most astonishing feature of these changes is the fact that, unlike other societal changes, transformations in gender relations have managed to pass by virtually unnoticed. Risseeuw turns to Bourdieu for theoretical assistance in explaining the silent character of this 'counter-revolution' in sexual politics. This enables her to analyze gender relations and their transformation as something outside the orthodoxy of what could be discussed in Sri Lanka at that particular moment in history.

Conclusion

The feminist project seems to have come full circle. It began with a rather simplified notion of power as oppression. Asymmetrical relations between the sexes were viewed as the inevitable artefact of patriarchal structures of domination. Women were lumped together, united in the universal sisterhood of oppression. In this monolithic perspective of male oppressors and female victims, resistance could only be effected by a joining of forces.

Despite its merits, the oppression paradigm of power had several serious drawbacks. It implied that it might be possible to develop one theory which would meet the requirements of the analysis of gender relations in all contexts, for all women and at all levels of social life. By focusing on global explanations for the shared feminine predicament, it became increasingly problematic to give due recognition to the diversity and complexity of women's experiences.

Moreover, it became increasingly difficult to conceptualize 'women', let alone the feminist subject, without falling into the concomitant trap of essentialism. The focus on collective struggle left little room to explore how women comply or resist, without ever reaching the point of collective mobilization. Since women seemed either to be knowledgeable or to be the victims of false consciousness, the nuances of awareness could not be conceptualized. As a consequence, the transformation of asymmetrical gender relations began to recede into the realm of science fiction. It was difficult to imagine how social change took place or, more important, why it did not.

The essays in this volume attempt to alleviate the pitfalls of the oppression model of gender relations by drawing upon contemporary theories of power. They provide a corrective to feminist gender theory which does not explicitly conceptualize power while, at the same time, pinpointing some of the difficulties involved in the study of power and gender in concrete social and historical contexts. Moreover, they place several questions squarely on the feminist agenda. For example, the conceptualization of power, particularly in intimate relations in informal or private contexts, is clearly a subject which requires further investigation. The relationship between agency and structure needs to be dealt with if theories of power are to have strategic value for feminists. We need to develop ways of retrieving women as political subjects while, at the same time, coming to terms with the structuration of social relations of power. Long-term processes of social change also pose special problems for the study of gender transformation. Power resources are clearly not straightforward when it comes to gender relations. This necessitates a careful sorting out of what happens when women use them.

In short, contemporary social theory can prove useful for feminist studies on power in gender relations. This is not, however, the end of the story. We need to continue thinking about how gender can be integrated into existing theoretical frameworks as well as how our gender theories can take account of the workings of power. Specific studies indicate that the relationship between power and gender is far from simple. Further reflection and the careful investigation of power in the concrete practices and contexts of women and men is clearly in order.

PART ONE

THREE DIMENSIONS OF POWER

1
Power and Love: Conflicting Conceptual Schemata

JOAN MEYER

> Feminists have dismissed romanticism, yet it has a
> psychic reality that can't simply be banished. The
> magic of dominance and sub-mission is written into
> romance as it is written into pornography; romance *is*
> actually a sort of pornography of the feelings, in which
> emotions replace sexual parts, yet may be just as
> fetishized. (Wilson 1986)

Power in loving relationships is not comparable to power in
other relationships, in that loving relations are vehicles of
both love and power at the same time. Therefore, in order
to understand the loving relationships most women have
with men as fathers, husbands, lovers, brothers and sons,
it is essential to include dimensions of both power and love
in any theory of relationships.[1]

Relationships between people are complex, multifaceted,
full of ambivalence and contradictions. On the one hand,
they do not remain constant, but tend to change over time.
On the other hand, relationships often manifest themselves
in various subtle, unnoticeable ways as relatively constant
and unchanging. What is taken by the partners to be a new
development in their relationship may be just more of the
same in another form. Modern Western culture has
devised ways of dealing with these confusing and kaleido-

scopic properties of relationships. At the everyday level these range from the fairy tale in infancy to Shakespeare and soap operas in later life. Social norms help regulate and order the emotional turmoil: there is a 'right' time, place and face for most feelings.

At the level of social science, a similar problem of bringing order into chaos manifests itself. Scientists have the task of describing a reality more complex than their own theories. In part, the process of theory building has followed paths already established by the structure of society in general. This has led to constraints on theorizing about relationships, reducing the value of the contributions of social science to everyday thinking, especially for women.

In this chapter, I shall provide a number of instances showing the interconnection of power and love in relationships, particularly at the level of culture. The question that I will seek to answer is: how has culture managed the power and love aspects of relations between men and women? In what ways have people been influenced by social structures and how have they, in turn, influenced those structures? In the second part of the chapter, I shall criticize feminist theory for focusing only on the oppressive nature of relationships. Feminist theorizing has primarily served to facilitate a process of consciousness-raising concerning power in relationships between the sexes. Useful and necessary as this function has been, and still is, to many women, it is necessary to move beyond the phase of unmasking oppression. It is time to develop new ways of conceptualizing relationships, incorporating more of the naturally existing ambivalences and dynamic aspects and offering more promising ways of dealing with relationships in everyday life. To this end I wish to examine the potential of Lukes' power theory as a descriptive meta-theory for relationships. I hope to show that this power theory offers a framework that can be used to integrate the two dimensions, power and love.

The dichotomy between love and power

Traditionally, Western culture has posed the concepts of power and love as a dichotomy, if not a contradiction. Power is a notion that belongs to the outside world, the public sphere. The exercise of power is associated with violence, self-interest, ambition, conflict and repression. Love belongs to the private realm of interpersonal relationships. It brings out the best in us; we associate love with selflessness, harmony, spiritual and emotional growth, intimacy, and sharing.

The nature of this contradiction is a cultural 'given': the unimpeded wielding of power by the powerful demands a certain detachment toward 'inferiors', hampered, however, by the salience of emotional and affectional ties. Those wishing to exercise power strive to maintain a physical and emotional distance from those they want to influence (Mulder 1972). Some of the strategies used by the less-powerful party in a power relation draw directly on these conflicting impulses: tactics of submission (also prevalent in the animal world) tend to block the successful execution of aggressive power maneuvers. The same holds true for some of the forms of referent power that Western culture traditionally allows women (Johnson 1978). The helplessly smiling female constitutes an appeal that (still) elicits benevolent compliance from the dominant male.

In the public sphere of power, love is supposed to be either out of place or irrelevant. The cultural taboo against mixing power with love is reflected in the segregation of the sexes in the world of work, in the way love affairs between bosses and employees tend to cause trouble and in the upheaval brought about by the 'scandalous' love affairs of politicians, which would be all too commonplace in other people's lives. It seems that love can be dangerous to power. People with widely disparate power positions create 'time-out' from power imbalances by falling in love. The love ideology, with its emphasis on giving, sharing and mutuality, declares power relations irrelevant. This could be termed the revolutionary power of love. Social and psychological gaps between those of unequal status, ethnic minorities and majorities, oppressors and oppressed, competing political and religious factions and men and women can be bridged by the simple power of love. It is no coincidence that societies seeking to preserve the power differential between subdivisions of the population discourage the forming of love ties between members of different groups. Whereas cultural or ethnic intermingling through ties of love can, in time, help to break down barriers, they seem to have the opposite effect in relationships between men and women.

In the late sixties and early seventies transgressions in the normative boundaries between love and power were prevalent. On the one hand, social groups like the hippies challenged the existing power structures in society by declaring that 'love is the only power' and adopting 'flower power' as a name for this movement. Thus, at least in their slogans, they used 'love' as a public and political strategy (Haley 1969). On the other hand, feminists in the wake of the second wave of feminism launched their attacks on the male–female love relationship stating that this relationship was corrupted by power inequalities. The breakdown of the taboo on connecting love and power, posing the question of what power does to love and vice versa, prepared the ground for the consciousness-raising movement and theoretical analyses of the institutions of marriage and motherhood.

Although both feminism and the hippie movement undermined the love/power dichotomy to some extent, other aspects remained intact. Love was seen as a political force to replace or supplant the power structure ('If everybody could just trust and love one another, there would be no need for . . .') and power differentials involved in male–female love relationships were still regarded as invalidating the love content ('All these years with X he was merely exploiting me'). A model for relationships that incorporated both power and love in an integrated fashion was still non-existent.

Transition

Our early experiences of love and power fail to conform to the culturally demanded segregation: the first relationship with beloved caretakers shows alternating modes of absolute power and powerlessness. As we develop a conception of ourself as a separate, autonomous person we start forming affectional ties of another nature with our peers. But the older forms retain a certain attraction and occasionally manifest themselves in 'crushes' on important teachers, or in love affairs with bosses, doctors and other powerful figures (Meyer 1983).

Current literature describing women's reactions to the discovery of oppression in long-term male–female relationships is strangely reminiscent of adolescence: protest, upheaval, recriminations, and finally 'leaving home' are common patterns (Schwarzer 1974; Bonte Was 1976; Rubin 1985). Just as the context of a love relationship obscured the power aspects of the relationship in the beginning, the power interpretation seemed to destroy or enervate any bonds of affection later on. The either/or dichotomy appears to be necessary for dealing with the complexities of multidimensional relations.

Simple models can be useful. Bettelheim argues convincingly that fairy tales with their extremes of good and bad characters provide a means for children to come to terms with their own inner dilemmas. Since children, like all of us, have a welter of contradictory feelings and have not yet learned to deal with these contradictions, they experience the mixtures of love and hate, desire and fear within themselves as an incomprehensible and frightening chaos. The images in fairy tales are essentially one-dimensional.

They help the child to sort out complex and ambivalent feelings by isolating and separating disparate and confusing aspects of the child's experience into opposites and projecting these onto different figures (Bettelheim 1977). As Bettelheim points out, even Freud found no better way to help make sense of this mixture of contradictions which coexists in our inner life than by creating symbols for isolated aspects of the personality. Id, superego and ego ideals are mere symbols, but none the less useful tools for sorting out and comprehending mental processes.

Feminist social scientists used similar techniques when they exposed the normative and ideological underpinnings of power between the sexes. The original feminist counter-theories devised to help women sort out the confusing tangle of their relationships with the male world made use of principles similar to the fairy tale: opposites were isolated and projected onto different figures, in this case, males and females. During this process, people taking more differentiated views were suspect. The use of extremes was required to create psychological distance between women's new interpretations of the world and themselves, and interpretations woven into the culture, confronting them daily still.

In adult life notions of good and bad, so prevalent in fairy tales, tend to go out of fashion. It still requires considerable energy to grasp emotionally, however, that we ourselves as well as others around us usually are both good and bad simultaneously. Moreover, in times of great emotional stress and crisis, we tend to revert to archaic and simplistic modes of managing our experience. At the peak of a separation or divorce, many women (and men) tend to make, as in a fairy tale, an all-powerful, all-evil figure of the person who was most likely enveloped in almost mythical goodness at another time (falling in love is another period of emotional turmoil).

Undoubtedly, the image of the Big Bad Wolf is functional when trying to sever the root and fibre that have intertwined in a long-term relationship. Blocking out good with evil can prevent vacillation between staying and leaving. Once the parting has been firmly established, the ex-partner can resume human proportions (Weiss 1975). However, the use of these primitive modes during crises illustrates the difficulty of integrating the notions of good and bad in our conception of one person. Similarly, it is difficult to conceive of a loving relationship that is simultaneously a power struggle. Interpretation tends to fluctuate between the two dimensions. This principle has also been used by social scientists, who have rarely gone beyond alternating modes to achieve integration. Let me give some examples:

In the Christian religion, love of God provides the context in which we interpret the story of the life of Jesus. A startling and to some people even shocking and innovative effect was achieved when Haley (1969) reinterpreted the events, actions and sayings of his life history from a power perspective. The sensation caused by this essay derives directly from our internalized norms regarding the mutual exclusiveness of love and power ('If it was power, it cannot have been love' and vice versa).

Nancy Henley achieved a similar effect when she reinterpreted non-verbal behavior popularly associated with intimacy, such as seeking proximity, gazing directly into someone's eyes and touching, from a power perspective. She documented her propositions with research showing that the behavior of men to women paralleled the behavior of higher status persons to lower status persons and vice versa. In other words, these forms of non-verbal behavior were shown to be instrumental in maintaining the power differential between the sexes (Henley 1977). In my own research I was able to demonstrate instances of this process of fluctuating between two modes of interpretation (Meyer 1983). Similar patterns of extreme dominance and submission in verbal and non-verbal behavior between a man and a woman were interpreted completely differently, depending on the situational context. When the situation was work-related (i.e. more business-like and associated with the public sphere), dominant behavior of both males and, to a slightly lesser extent, females was interpreted in a power frame of reference and condemned. If similar behavior was presented as occurring in the context of a party (i.e. conducive to the formation of interpersonal relationships and, therefore, more associated with the private sphere), it was interpreted as a romantic overture and approved. This occurred in spite of the fact that the subjects all belonged to a group with extremely liberal views regarding the position of women in society.

Power theories in social psychology

Power is a relatively neglected topic in social psychology. Feminist theorists, seeking to understand the dynamics of the male–female power process, have not found much help in traditional theorizing. A number of factors have given rise to this situation. First of all, most theories used metaphors chosen for their supposedly value-free format: for example, the metaphor of the marketplace or of bodily homeostasis (Gergen 1980). The choice of 'value-free' metaphors has obscured the political nature of power, the fact that power has to do with differences of interest.

Secondly, to translate the principles of these metaphors into social relations, theorists have usually relied heavily on the laws, structures and processes operating in typically male institutions like the army, the football club and formal political or labor organizations. The modeling on traditionally male institutions has removed women and issues related to love, intimacy and sexuality from the agenda of power. Power is reduced to a contest between men in the public sphere, keeping well within the bounds of what is considered proper and appropriate in these areas. What happens in between the rounds of formal contest is declared irrelevant.

Finally, as Moscovici (1976) points out, studies of social influence have traditionally concentrated on the reasons why people conform as well as on successful means to make them conform. The perspective is that of the leader or leader-to-be (Meyer 1983). By this choice of perspective, the origin of change, influence exerted by the less-powerful participants in the relationship and the shifting of the power balance are all removed from the agenda. Since it is exactly this perspective that inspired feminist theorists in the first place to take an interest in questions of power, such theories have little to offer them.

The biases in theorizing illustrate the circular processes of domination: who funds the research, who determines, formulates or approves the questions posed? Perspectives relevant to the less-powerful groups did not emerge until much later and can be seen as the result of social changes. A case in point is the classic experiment of Solomon Asch on conformity (Asch 1956).

In this experiment, a subject is confronted with unequivocal stimuli (for example, lines of equal length) in a group situation. The other group members are stooges, instructed to give the same false answer unanimously. Asch attempted to construct a rational theory of influence to counter existing doctrine on prestige suggestion. He hoped to prove that people in general act rationally and, therefore, expected his subject to disregard the false answers given by the other group members. In fact, his experiment proved what it set out to disprove. Most people will conform to group pressure, even if this means distorting their perceptions of objective reality. The outcome of this experiment was obviously of practical use for leaders intent upon finding 'tricks' for ruling the masses (Moscovici 1985).

When social developments caused those formerly considered deviant to take their place as active minorities, attempting to change society and its values, these same experiments were viewed from a different perspective. Moscovici (1976) used the same Asch experiments, but this time as a starting point from which to determine the conditions and ways in which an active minority could influence the majority. Thus, preoccupation with conformity was replaced by interest in change and innovation.

The relevance of Moscovici's shift in perspective is recognized in social psychology. However, important as this is, it has not been sufficient to stimulate the development of broader theories relevant to the power relation between the sexes. Subsequent work has been fragmented, mainly research-oriented and preoccupied with technological aspects of the relationship (for example, which button does one press to get reaction x?). To use the former metaphor: tricks for ruling the masses are being supplemented by tricks for resisting majority influence.

Power theories and gender

A theory of power relevant to less-powerful groups must incorporate mechanisms for change. Change has a different meaning, however, for different categories of powerlessness. The young white, male radical who criticizes existing doctrine and structure can use his minority position to become prominent. When the time comes, he can melt into the new generation of leaders and become part of the establishment, having done his bit for innovation. For those groups in society whose powerlessness is related to immediately recognizable physical attributes (women, ethnic minorities etc.), it is not enough to strive for individual or group power. They cannot become integrated and, subsequently, invisible in the powerful group. They will be repeatedly confronted with the fact that their actions are interpreted and valued in ways different from similar actions by members of the powerful group. Until they succeed in changing the power relation itself, they will experience the effects of inequality.

A theory of power that is relevant for women must, on the one hand, incorporate concepts which are employed to define the relative power position of women and the characteristics used to define the value attached to 'women' as a social category and, on the other hand, it must incorporate mechanisms of change, that is, be process-oriented.

To meet these demands it is necessary first of all to look at the way the relationship is described by the less-powerful party, women themselves. The women's move-ment has defined the intermingling of power and love relationships in the midst of a culture in which the dominant view is that power and love relationships are separate and belong to different realms as one of its central issues (Amsberg and Steenhuis 1982). Accounts given by rape victims show that most have little doubt about what happened to them. They describe themselves as victims of violent, aggressive crime, which befell them due to simple structures of male–female domination and the unhappy coincidence that they happened to be in a particular place at a particular time. There is no room for images of women as irresistible sources of fatal attraction that backfires. The long-term consequences, however, described by the women themselves, indicate that they have been hurt most in aspects of their personality which are essential for love, not power. Damage in terms of fear and loss of self-confidence weighs heavily because there is even greater damage in the areas of trust, giving and feeling free to enjoy one's body and one's sexuality.

The accounts of the victims of violent and sexual child abuse are even more poignant: it seems as if love itself has been raped. What is important from a theoretical point of view is that the child's love for its parents is abused and that this abuse is made possible by the extreme power differential involved. The tremendous amount of psychic and emotional energy required to overcome and process such experiences is only partly related to developing and becoming a person in one's own right. A much larger part is concerned with the damage in the sphere of love: will I ever be able to love another person freely, trustfully? Will I ever be able to have children and love them without fear for others or for myself? In unequal power relations, the more-powerful party tends to disregard the viewpoint of the less powerful. This holds true for male–female relationships, both at a macrosocial level and on an interpersonal basis. From a position of power it is attractive and easy to assume that others will go along with your preferences. Precisely this tendency has functioned to justify actions which harm women's interests: rape victims 'asked for it'. Children submitting to sexual abuse have been accused of leading the abuser on or of having fantasized the whole episode. Women categorically denied entrance to higher education and access to (well-)paid positions have been told, not only that these measures were designed with their best interests in mind ('for their own good'), but that they were conducive to the fulfillment of their 'more fundamental' wishes. After all, it is only the male who is 'instrumental' (read: interested in power), whereas the female is merely 'expressive' (read: interested in love).

Time and again, the preferences of the more-powerful party have been projected onto the less powerful, denying them a right to their own wishes, preferences and goals. The same mechanism might well be at work in theory building, making it dangerous to leave this activity to the more-powerful party in the relationship. In fact, it is easy enough to point out instances where these metamorphic aspects of power (Kipnis 1976) have influenced theorizing on relationships between women and men (Meyer 1983).

To conclude: a theory of relationships that does justice to women's own accounts and their concerns must be designed to give voice to the less-powerful party, and leave room for incorporating the positive feelings such as love, trust, affection. By treating power as a strictly 'business-like' concept, many issues relevant to women are removed from the discussion of power. The very definition of 'power' as a separate, somehow mysteriously distinct entity can be conceived as a way to delete love from the agenda, in keeping with viricentric cultural traditions. The view taken here is that to remain close to the accounts of women, power has to be defined as an aspect of relationships. The primary focus, whether at the interpersonal or group level or on a wider societal basis, should be on the relationship.

Toward a theory of relationships

A theory that uses the relationship as a central focus would avoid the fluctuations created by the cultural dichotomy of power and love. 'Power' is commonly taken to refer to conflicting interests and 'love' to presuppose mutual interests. From a perspective of relationships, however, it is both legitimate and relevant to ask to what extent a relationship is characterized by conflicting or mutual interests and in which areas. In everyday experience it is accepted that the same relationship can be beneficial in some areas and harmful in others.

Relationships are not expected to remain constant over time. Thus, a relational model must be process-oriented rather than static. Such a model also allows for both personal and impersonal aspects of relationships. It is essential that theory, relevant to relations between the sexes, leaves room for the – more impersonal – structural component of relationships. Many of the dilemmas involved in the 'power–love dichotomy' can be incorporated by focusing on the mutual and differential interests of parties in a dynamic relational context, including an analysis of structural aspects.

A political approach to power formulated by Steven

Lukes in 1974 became popular among Dutch feminist social scientists in the early eighties. Lukes' theory offers a possible framework for relational theory. The model leaves room for combining both personal and structural aspects of relationships. Since it is process-oriented and focuses on change, it seems a promising starting point for relational theory involving power and love.

Lukes' observations on power were first connected to relations between the sexes by Komter (1979). Römkens, Meyer and Komter have applied this theory to wife abuse, the interpretation of interaction and male–female relations in marriage, respectively (Römkens 1980; Meyer 1983; Komter 1985). Strictly speaking, Lukes' approach cannot be termed a theory, as it does not lead unequivocally to falsifiable predictions or testable hypotheses. Power is defined as both relative and a characteristic of relationships. Describing relationships in terms of this power perspective means questioning which party in a relationship has the greater potential to determine the behavior of the other party. If power is actualized, it is defined as control.

Since, in Lukes' view, power need not be intentional, the power perspective can be used not only to describe personal aspects of relations between people or groups, but also to describe structural or institutional aspects of relationships. Using a power perspective is conducive to change. An observation that A can determine B's behavior to a greater extent than vice versa can be followed by the question under which conditions this relationship is open to change. Behavior is used here in a broad sense, covering cognitions, acts and feelings.

Lukes describes three dimensions through which power operates, each suggesting a different strategy for identifying power relations. Each calls into question more social phenomena than the one before. First, 'one-dimensional' power is identified by looking at decision-making and comparing stated preferences to actual outcomes. Not all questions in which there is a conflict of interest, however, lead to decision-making. In some instances the powerful party in a relationship uses his or her power to keep important questions off the agenda. Thus, to find 'two-dimensional' power, the researcher should identify areas of 'non-decision-making' and look for grievances harbored by the less-powerful party in the relationship. The 'third dimension' of power, identified by Lukes, carries the argument yet a step further. Absence of grievances does not mean that power is not involved; the power relation could be latent. As Lukes states:

> Is it not the supreme and most insidious exercise of power to prevent people, to whatever degree, from having grievances, by shaping their perceptions, cognitions and preferences in such a way that they accept their role in the existing order of things, either because they can see or imagine no alternative to it, or because they see it as natural and unchangeable, or because they value it as divinely ordained and beneficial? (Lukes 1974: 24)

In a study of battered wives, Römkens describes what she calls the 'oh-but-he-needs-me syndrome'. This is an interpretation of the husbands' behavior that renders leaving them practically impossible for the women concerned. Thus, the three-dimensional view points to yet a third strategy, inducing the social scientist to look for interpretations of situations and relations that block alternatives (real or as yet imaginary) from view.

An attempt to adapt the principles formulated in Lukes' framework would define power as the relative contribution of parties involved to the end-product of an interaction.[2] From a one-dimensional perspective, the researcher can ask parties involved in a relationship to state what their preferences are, both in specific areas of the relationship and concerning the relationship *per se*. Stated preferences can then be related to actual outcomes. It is important to note that whereas from a power perspective only dissimilar preferences are of interest, from a relational point of view, both shared and dissimilar preferences are relevant. Comparison of shared and dissimilar preferences can show the way to ambivalence and tension, built into the relationship on an observable level. Dissimilar preferences point to the relative contributions of parties in a relationship. Shared preferences can bring to light obstructions in the environment, or at a different level of the relationship. For instance, both partners might strive toward an equal division of household work, but find it difficult to put this principle into practice due to constraints imposed by the environment, and habits acquired previously in the relationship.

From a two-dimensional perspective, the researcher can look for grievances and issues that one of the parties involved has been unable to place on the common agenda. In other words, which are the matters that one party desires to discuss or negotiate overtly but that subsequently fail to get discussed? At the personal level, grievances can be directed at the partner in the relationship. At the structural level, grievances can be directed at the institutional practices, norms and expectations regulating the relationship. This two-dimensional relational framework can incorporate traditional male–female relations as well as relations in which one or both parties are deliberately striving toward new, unorthodox forms. Taking the two-dimensional model as a guideline, the researcher could use grievances to point out areas that require negotiation. Separating the personal from the political makes it possible to identify the agendas within which issues can be dealt with. A successful discussion of grievances toward one's partner in the relationship would render the issue amenable to the treatment described under the one-dimensional approach: relating stated preferences to actual outcomes. The correct identification of issues as structural rather than personal would point to options for political action by the parties involved.

The three-dimensional approach concentrates on the interpretations used by the parties involved in the relationship. Interpretations can refer to the relationship *per se*, or to important areas or issues concerned in the relationship. For example, Komter in her research on married couples identified five main areas: sexuality, the children, work outside the home, work inside the home, and social contacts and leisure. The crucial question from a three-dimensional point of view is the availability of actual alternatives and the awareness of existing alternatives. To what extent are the views of one or both partners in the relationship characterized by a sense of inevitability? Up to a point, the researcher can strive to move issues from the three-dimensional sphere into the two- or one-dimensional sphere. This can be done by confronting subjects with alternatives, constructed on theoretical grounds, which remove actual or psychological obstacles. Specified variations of the general question 'What would you prefer if anything were possible?' are used: 'How would you react if your husband suddenly became a feminist?' 'What would your reaction be if the government passed a law enforcing communal childcare?' etc. However, the value of this approach for identifying preferences is limited if the options put before subjects have little or no psychological reality for them. In that case, subjects will probably reject the question. The grounds used for doing so ('He's too old to change'; 'Marriage just isn't like that') can, however, point to actual or psychological obstructions blocking alternatives.

If the object of the research is to expose structural aspects of relations, a second possible research strategy is based on the identification of 'inevitables' or 'unchangeables' in a relationship. Here, comparison groups with more options are used to bring preferences to light. This would mean a comparison of inevitables in different types of love relationship, for instance, combined with questions regarding preferences in relationships characterized by relatively few inevitables. Even in the same type of relationship, what is taken as given or inevitable may vary at different stages or different moments in time. For instance, in Komter's research among married couples with children, many of the men made statements regarding childcare to the effect that 'You just can't take the mother's place' (Komter 1985), whereas in my own study of parents-to-be a young man, when asked what kind of father he wanted to be, replied 'I want to be a mother'. He later stated that his wife and he had decided that he was going to fulfill the mother role (Meyer forthcoming).

Another limitation of questions which, in effect, ask 'What would you prefer if anything were possible?' is the possibility that in some very unequal power relations such questions can be threatening to the subject's psychological equilibrium. To give an extreme example: in the case of child abuse, a question implying the removal of the abusive parent from the home could be dangerous to the child, since fear of losing the parent or of disrupting the relationship between parents is part of the problem. In that case, the researcher has no alternative but to look for comparison groups where the abusive parent has actually been removed from the child's life, and in this case to interview independent adults about their interpretation of the abusive relationship, in retrospect. From a relational perspective one would strive to interview the abusive parent as well. Although there are studies of abusive parents, these are usually treated as a separate category, and studied by other researchers specializing in that aspect of the problem. I have not come across studies that deal with the relation from both vantage points.

In the relational model described above, a powerful position is one in which more stated preferences are realized, fewer grievances are harbored and fewer aspects of the relationship are interpreted as inevitable or unchangeable. Conversely, a relatively powerless position is reflected in the presence of many unchangeables or inevitables in the description of issues or areas of the relationship, relatively more grievances harbored when inevitability is suspended and a weak relation between stated preferences and actual outcomes.

Conclusion

In this chapter, I have taken the descriptive narratives of women concerning problematic aspects of their relationships with men as a point of reference. What appears to be specific to intimate relations is that, while they can be viewed as power relations, at the same time they invite affection between members of less-powerful and more-powerful groups. Current theory does not lend itself to incorporating love and power in the same model. In Western cultural tradition there is a dichotomy between the notions of power and love. Social science has failed to challenge this dichotomy.

One of the ways in which the slogan of the women's movement in the sixties, 'the personal is political', can be interpreted is as follows: during this period women started to realize that the decisions and choices they made in their personal lives, based mainly on affective and personal considerations, had political consequences on a larger social scale. Personal choices and decisions followed common patterns to the extent that they conformed to structural demands. Moreover, the options presenting themselves for choice were predetermined at the political level.

From this perspective, it seems fitting that political theory be adapted so as to be relevant to the sphere of personal relationships. Relational theory could show how models might incorporate both aspects without confusing the issues at stake. The theoretical model described, developed from political theory, is inherently suited to bring to light options for change and political action.

In order to avoid the creation of new dichotomies, both mutual and different interests are deemed relevant. Taking both into account does justice to the ambivalent and contradictory nature of intimate male–female relationships. Since in everyday experience the structural and the personal are intertwined, social science could help distinguish what is part of a common cultural 'given' (not necessarily unchangeable but calling for different strategies of change) from personal wishes and ideals.

In the social psychological literature on love relationships, it appears that the interpretations and definitions being used to describe relationships vary considerably: companionate love, passionate love, attachment, romantic love, friendship, altruistic love etc. Furthermore, in actual, continuing relationships, interpretations of the relationship move through various stages as perceived by the people involved: as relationships grow closer, people feel increasingly that their interests are inextricably tied to the well-being of the relationship (Berscheid 1985). A developmental or process-oriented model seems essential, if we are to do justice to the ways in which people involved in a relationship experience it, as well as to the ways in which the power differential is maintained or changed.

It seems to me that the most important contribution of Lukes' power theory lies in the shift away from mere decision-making to the actual content of relationships as defined by the participants. Relational dynamics can largely be understood in these terms, since the definition of the relationship shapes the interpetation of what follows, including decision-making. This holds true on a macrosocial level, for instance if countries define the action of a nation as 'aggression' rather than 'protection' or 'self-defense'. It is especially apt in interpersonal relations, where negotiations as to the content can be conceived as a continuing discussion taking place in everyday life. The statement: 'I love you' is not a factual observation. It is an invitation to define or redefine the content of the relationship.

Depending on the answer ('I know you do', '. . . ahm, I'm very fond of you my dear', 'What can I say?' 'I love you too, but I'd love you even better if you didn't . . .' or, simply, 'I love you'), different scenarios ensue, with widely disparate emotional content and varying power differentials. And for those of whom no answer is expected, even such a seemingly benign statement can sound like the door of a prison cell closing.

Notes

1 Obviously, power is involved in relations between women as well. In this paper, the focus is on gender relations involving love. However, many of the points I will be making also apply to relationships between women.
2 As in all relational theory, punctuation is essentially arbitrary, but must be specified in concrete instances (Watzlawick et al. 1967).

2
Gender, Power and Feminist Theory
AAFKE KOMTER

The view that gender relations are characterized by power seems to have been generally endorsed within feminism in recent years. However, opinions differ on the implications of this view for feminist theorizing. Do we have to develop a feminist theory of power and gender, or can we resort to existing social theory to explain the gendered consequences of power? This question is related to the development of feminist theorizing in general. During the past two decades, feminist thought has displayed a rather strong tendency toward general theories and explanatory principles: theoretical approaches explaining all we had always wanted to know about women and men and their problematic relationship. Although the terms and concepts used to explain the feminist problematic have varied greatly – oppression, relations of production and reproduction, the sex-class system, capitalist patriarchy, the sex-gender system, the phallus, mothering, discourse, construction, power – the underlying tendency to resort to one main theoretical principle is similar.

Interestingly, the object of women's studies seems, at the same time, to have entered a severe crisis. Paradoxes, dilemmas and ambiguities are seen everywhere. The category 'women' has lost its former clarity; pluriformity, multiplicity and diversity of meaning dominate the scene in feminist theorizing. Rosalind Delmar describes one of the main paradoxes of recent feminism as follows:

although it started on the terrain of sexual antagonism between men and women, it moved quickly to a state in which relations between women caused the most internal stress. Women, in a sense, are feminism's greatest problem. (Delmar 1986: 27–28)

In this chapter, I want to explore the question of whether attempts at developing a general feminist theory of gender and power can be considered a fruitful scientific enterprise. In the first section I shall make a short expedition into the recent history of feminist theorizing. From this history I will be arguing, in the second section, that general approaches to feminist theory are doomed to fail. Finally, the possibility of using existing social theory on power for feminist analyses will be discussed. As an example, I will present the theoretical framework of my research on marital power, which was based on Steven Lukes' concept of power (1974), and Gramsci's notion of ideological hegemony (1971). I will conclude that specific approaches to power, borrowed from existing social theory, can offer some insight into specific areas of feminist concern.

Recent history of feminist theory

In the early seventies several calls were heard for a general theory of women's oppression. Several currents, differing greatly in their political and strategic perspectives, had developed within the feminist movement. Theoretically, however, these were often based on the same source of inspiration: Marxism. Although there were many differences between radical and Marxist feminism, the radical feminists' analysis in terms of the 'sex-class system' (e.g. Firestone 1971), as well as the focus of socialist feminists on the (inter)relationships of reproduction and production – or 'capitalist patriarchy' (e.g. Eisenstein 1979) – displayed a common heritage: the kind of political analysis that had become popular in the leftist movement during the sixties.

The Marxist heritage became particularly prominent in the so-called 'domestic labor debate'. The central concern of this debate was the effort to model the analysis of domestic labor on the general Marxist analysis of the exchange of value in the labor market. The debate – a real intellectual *tour de force* – illustrated that a good match between Marxism and feminism was, at the time, considered to be of paramount importance.

Later, this marriage came increasingly to be seen as an unhappy one (Hartmann 1979b), and there were pleas for a more or less strict divorce (Aerts 1981; Outshoorn 1981). Experiences in the women's movement had pointed to the need to differentiate within the category 'women'. The early analyses, which took the sex-class system or capitalist patriarchy as their main theoretical focus, proved too monolithic and failed to account for the ways in which women are differentiated by political, cultural and sexual loyalties and by racial, class and ethnic identities. Moreover, the Marxist approach – with its economic overtones – did not prove to be very promising where a theoretical understanding of issues like sexuality or motherhood was concerned. The marriage of feminism and Marxism contained the germs of a process which was to split theoretical feminism into several, often rival feminisms. This would eventually have devastating consequences for relational happiness.

Among feminists a growing need to account for the ideological and psychological dimensions of gender inequality was felt, especially with respect to the issues of reproduction and sexuality. This need pointed toward a new, potentially interesting marital partner, one who was both attractive and authoritative: psychoanalysis. Psychoanalysis was expected to offer a theory regarding the genesis of masculine and feminine subjectivity.

Authors such as Juliet Mitchell, Gayle Rubin and Nancy

Chodorow stimulated important new understandings of the psychological and ideological complexities of femininity, masculinity and gender relationships. They drew attention to the ways in which gendered identity comes into being in the context of the system of primary bonds and relations that is most often synonymous with 'the family' in Western culture.

But the marriage between feminism and psychoanalysis also became strained as it appeared to possess a multiple personality: part Lacanian (Mitchell 1974), and part inspired by the psychoanalytic tradition of object relationships (Chodorow 1978). Both feminism and psychoanalysis shared a tendency to universals such as castration and the Oedipus complex, but the results of their thinking pointed in quite different directions. In the first approach, the gendered implications of the phallus as the signifying symbol in Western culture were stressed, particularly the fundamentally different ways in which women and men are inserted into Western culture. The second approach, which is most clearly represented by the work of Nancy Chodorow, emphasized mothering as the structuring principle of gender identity and gender relationships.

Serious marital disputes began to overshadow the relationship between feminism and psychoanalysis. The overpowering impact of the symbol of the phallus appeared a difficult premise to explain from within Lacanian thought and Chodorow's stress on the universality of the sex-linked psychosocial consequences of mothering came under severe attack. Moreover, she was accused of neglecting the essence of psychoanalytical theory – the unconscious – by transforming it into a 'socialization theory', a genre which seems since to have fallen into disrepute. The introduction of psychonalysis into feminist theory had given new fuel to the growing theoretical fragmentation within feminism.

The marriage of feminism with Marxism and psycho-analysis, respectively, had brought to light two serious problems. On the one hand, there was the discovery of the illusion of a 'given' feminine subject. The other related problem was that the stability of the object of feminism – once unproblematically defined as 'women's oppression' – began to crumble. Not only was the theoretical or analytical usefulness of the concept of 'women's oppression' questioned, but one also began to wonder what feminism really was (Mitchell and Oakley 1986). These developments can be seen as a reflection of the growing fragmentation of the women's movement as a political movement.

The ground seemed prepared for new amorous adventures for feminist theory. Fierce debates followed about which theoretical suitor would make the best match. The time seemed ripe for a lover capable of annihilating the last remains of the illusion of the feminine subject as a fixed entity, thereby stimulating a new series of questions about what the object of feminism might be. A suitable candidate was found in the discourse analysis inspired by Foucault. This approach focuses in particular on the socially constructed character of 'femininity' and relies heavily on notions of discursive power. Another line of thought also focuses on power, but differs from discourse analysis in many respects. In a sense this approach builds on the old idea of 'oppression' by emphasizing gender as a relationship which is fundamentally structured by power. I shall now briefly discuss these two lines of theory.

In the discourse perspective, femininity is seen as constructed by a discursive plurality of positions. No fixed meanings can be discerned in categories like sexuality, sex, gender, femininity or masculinity. Research should concentrate on the manifold ways in which meaning is produced with respect to these categories and on the mechanisms of power that play a role in this process. Whereas in the past feminism had concentrated on the study of the consequences of power inequality in gender relationships, discourse analysis shifted attention to its premises: what is gender anyway? If something like gender exists, how is it constructed? How can we talk of inequality when the category 'women' has no fixed meaning?

Although all reference to universals and general explanatory principles seems to be absent in Foucault – 'femininity' and 'women' are associated with ever-shifting meanings and a plurality of differences – a new general explanation has secretly invaded feminist thinking: the power of discourse. This power is assumed to be omnipresent and omnipotent. As a consequence, every social phenomenon or event is regarded from the point of view of its discursive construction.

These assumptions of discourse analysis point to three specific problems for feminism. In the first place, due to its emphasis on the universal power of discourse and the resulting fundamental diversity and ambiguity of meaning, terms like 'gender' and 'femininity' seem to lose their conceptual meaning altogether, as no definable referent seems to be accepted. The idea of a socially constructed gender and of 'women' as an underprivileged social category runs the risk of being swallowed up in the bottomless swamp of permanently shifting meanings and ambivalent discursive constructions. The rigorous anti-essentialism displayed in some writings of this genre can literally cause speechlessness, as is, perhaps, best illustrated by the short life granted the British journal *M/F*.

A second problem is that Foucault-inspired discourse analysis seems to concentrate particularly on the concepts of 'femininity' and 'women'. As a consequence, the relevance of women's studies of the concepts 'masculinity' and 'men', as well as their relationships to the first set of concepts, may get out of sight.

A third problematic aspect of discourse analysis is its underlying view of human beings. Although it is certainly true that human beings are permanently involved in the production or reproduction of meaning, too strong a fixation on the constructed character of social reality may lead to a lack of attention to other relevant characteristics of human beings like, for example, their 'agency' and capacity to transform social reality by giving it new meaning or intervening in social practices.

In recent years, discourse analysis has become a satisfying and powerful lover of some segments of European and American feminism. Other segments, however, feel more attracted to a different, but increasingly popular theoretical perspective: power. Among the many feminists who consider power to be a promising theoretical approach to gender is Nancy Hartsock (1983). Several Dutch feminist scholars have also been using the concept of power in their research, trying to explain, for example, medical encounters (Davis 1988b) or marital power (Komter 1985, 1989a). However, their approach differs from the one Hartsock propagates, in that they use power as a specific analytical tool for a specific purpose, not as a general concept for feminist theory.

Hartsock, then, has attempted to develop a general feminist theory on gender, power and class. Expanding and modifying Marxist analysis, she proposes a theory that can encompass the gender as well as the class dimensions of relations of domination. She points to the ways in which Eros and power have been connected in the contemporary Western world and have structured gender relationships. The erotic dimension of power has taken the form of opposition and domination. Hartsock argues that the gender related to power associates masculinity with domination and, by means of this connection, fuses sexuality, violence and death. Moreover, the material life of women and men is structured in fundamentally opposing ways, as is demonstrated by the sexual division of labor. In her analysis Hartsock proposes to 'lay aside the important differences among women and instead to search for central commonalities across race and class boundaries' (1983: 233). In her view of power, one party is always exercising power at the expense of the other. Men and women 'share no common interest, and experience each other as threats to continued existence' (1983: 178).[1]

Unfortunately, Hartsock's theoretical account seems to suffer from the same tendency toward universalism displayed in the Marxist, psychoanalytic and discourse analyses discussed above. Her perspective implies that it is impossible to conceive simultaneously of women as a socially constructed gender and a category involving different sexual, social, political and cultural loyalties. Moreover, her assumptions about the fundamental opposition of interests of women and men as well as the concomitant, unilateral power relationships between them reflect a contestable conception of power as exclusively oppressive and based on conflict. Finally, she gives a rather stereotyped account of the ways women and men are supposed to experience and express Eros and the social consequences of this.

Problems with general feminist theory

Whereas the theoretical approaches within feminism discussed here have extremely divergent results, they all share a strong tendency toward general explanations. Both the tendency to overlook differences (as in the Marxist, psychoanalytical and some of the power approaches) and the tendency to over-accentuate them (as in discourse analysis) are consequences of the 'universalistic' pretensions and character of the analytical perspectives employed within feminism. Explanations of gender in terms of relations of (re)production, the feminine position with respect to the phallus, the social construction of femininity or a unilateral power relationship can only offer interpretations of social reality at a very global level; they can in no way be substituted for a more detailed theoretical and empirical analysis.

For example, it has been stated repeatedly from a

psychoanalytic perspective that a description of the different ways in which women and men are inserted into the symbolic order provides a theory about the genesis of femininity in our culture. Feminists who endorse discourse analysis demonstrate again and again that femininity is a discursive construction and that sexual identity is not 'given' but socially constructed. Although these broad statements are certainly not incorrect, they are not very enlightening when it comes to particular aspects in the lives of specific women or to knowing how these aspects are related to 'social constructions'.

The main problem with these theoretical approaches is that both the explanandum ('gender', 'femininity') and the explanans (e.g. 'social constructions') are formulated in terms which lack theoretical differentiation and empirical specificity. As a consequence, these approaches run the risk of fruitlessly repeating themselves without providing any new insights.

In the past few years, consciousness of the limitations of general theories seems to have been growing (e.g. Eisenstein and Jardine 1987; Segal 1987). Currently, however, general theoretical accounts of the genesis and production of concepts like 'gender' or 'femininity' have become rather popular within feminism. Current developments such as the feminist debate about 'equality and difference' (see, for example, Sommer 1985; Aerts 1986a; Komter 1988; Scott 1988; Riley 1988) might be regarded as related to the earlier attempts at general feminist theory.

Apart from the problems mentioned above, there are more specific theoretical arguments against a general feminist theory regarding gender and power. I see two kinds of arguments against such a theory. The first argument pertains to what I consider to be the main theoretical characteristics of gender. In the second argument, some theoretical characteristics of power in social relationships, including gender relations, are dealt with.

An exclusive concentration on 'women' and 'men' as

opposed social categories, as encountered in Marxist, psychoanalytical and power approaches, does not do justice to the diversity of gender relations. On the other hand, an exclusive focus on difference and diversity within the category 'women', as in discourse analysis, tends to ignore the fact that the relation between the sexes is fundament- ally determined by power. This perceptual incongruity might be compared with the famous picture representing at the same time a vase and a woman's face: one sees either one or the other, but never both at the same time. However, this incongruity is only apparent. The two perspectives on gender are not mutually exclusive, although this has often been suggested. In the words of Nancy Cott:

> Feminist stress on women's socially constructed 'difference' from men can go along with recognition of diversity among women themselves, if we acknowledge the multifaceted entity – the patchwork quilt, so to speak – that is the group called women. (Cott 1986: 50–60)

I would argue, then, that general theoretical approaches to 'gender' or 'femininity', whether inspired by Marxism, psychoanalysis, discourse analysis or power, are not very useful for a better understanding of either the regularities or the multifaceted character of gender relationships. The fact that both between-sex differences and within-sex differences are crucially important for feminist analysis should serve instead as an argument against any general feminist theory, including one based on power.

But there is another argument for refraining from the effort of developing a feminist theory of power and gender. This argument pertains to the similarities between power in gender relations and power in other kinds of social relations.

One could argue that gender, class and ethnicity are the most fundamental social criteria on which power inequality is based. This raises the question of what similarities or differences exist among these types of power relations as well as what conclusions can be drawn concerning the way in which power in gender relations might be conceptualized. To begin with, power relations arising from gender, ethnicity and class have a number of characteristics in common:

1   inequality in social resources, social position, political and cultural influence;
2   inequality in opportunities to make use of existing resources;
3   inequality in the division of rights and duties (cf. Schuyt 1973);
4   inequality in implicit or explicit standards of judgement, often leading to differential treatment (in laws, the labor market, educational practices etc.);
5   inequality in cultural representations: devaluation of the powerless group, stereotyping, references to the 'nature' or (biological) 'essence' of the less powerful;
6   inequality in psychological consequences: a 'psychology of inferiority' (insecurity, 'double-bind' experiences, and sometimes identification with the dominant group) versus a 'psychology of superiority' (arrogance, inability to abandon the dominant perspective);
7   social and cultural tendency to minimize or deny power inequality: (potential) conflict often represented as consensus, power inequality as 'normal'.

Of course, there are also differences in power relations based on gender, ethnicity or class. For example, one might wonder if 'typically feminine' experiences such as biological and social reproduction should be taken as an argument justifying the need for a general feminist theory about gender and power. Love and dependency in heterosexual relations might also be seen as necessitating the development of such a theory. Furthermore, phenomena such as

sexual abuse of women, pornography, prostitution and
violence against women might be regarded as reasons for a
general feminist theory of gender and power.

It is my contention that none of these experiences or
phenomena offers the 'decisive argument'. Of course,
reproduction and heterosexual love distinguish gender
relations from other social relations involving power.
There is, however, no *a priori* reason to assume that power
in gender relations works in a different way or has
fundamentally different consequences from other power
relations. Power in heterosexual relations might even be
regarded as a prototype of the way in which general
characteristics of power may be manifested.

Although sexual exploitation, slavery and violence are
quite typical of male–female relations, they are not limited
to these relations, but may also figure in same–sex relations.
Here again, there does not seem to be a fundamental
difference in the way power functions in the two types of
relations. I would argue, then, that power in gender
relations is not fundamentally different – neither in its
workings, nor in its social consequences – from power in
other kinds of social relations. Although the conditions and
circumstances of power inequality in gender relations are
different from those in which power develops in other
social relations, the mechanisms of power, its sociocultural
manifestations and its social consequences, are likely to be
similar.

These two arguments against a general feminist theory
of power and gender do not imply that there is no need for
feminist theorizing about power and gender whatsoever.
However, it should not aim at giving one general theoretical
account of power in gender relations. 'Gender' or 'femininity' are too varied and too complex to be explained by one
single theoretical principle. Rather, I would claim, as Davis
does in this book, that theories adequate for explaining
specific practices where power and gender are intertwined
will prove to be more helpful in the long run, when

combined with detailed empirical analyses. When undertaking such an effort, it is quite possible to make use of existing social theory on power. In doing so, however, it will be necessary in most cases to reformulate the theory from a feminist viewpoint and adapt it to one's specific research aims. Many social theories on power are flawed by implicit or explicit sexism and they all display blind spots where gender is concerned.

I will now illustrate my claim that existing social theory can be productively used in a feminist analysis of power and gender, using my research on power in marital relationships as an example.

Existing social theory on power and feminist analysis

In my own research I examined marriage as a specific locus of power (Komter 1985). The question as to which theory to use was not a simple one, because existing theories on marital power had some severe shortcomings. In their well-known study, *Husbands and Wives*, Blood and Wolfe (1960) had laid the basis for a tradition of research into marital power in which decision-making was the main indicator. The focus on observable, behavioral outcomes of power, operationalized as conflicts over decisions, diverted attention from the underlying power processes. The structural character of the unequal division of power resources between women and men was overlooked. Women and men were generally seen as having equal chances of getting the most advantageous outcomes in their negotiations on important marital matters, and their resources were considered as equivalent. Despite manifold criticisms, the outcome of decision-making is still considered the primary indicator of marital power (McDonald 1980: 846), and underlying structural inequality remains underestimated.

My research on marital power focused on power mechanisms and processes rather than their outcomes. The concept of power of Steven Lukes (1974) seemed a useful starting point because of the attention it pays to ideological and structural power. Lukes (1974) distinguishes three perspectives on power. The so-called one-dimensional view is historically rooted in Max Weber's concept of power. Weber defined power as the ability to enforce one's will, even against resistance. Studies carried out from a one-dimensional perspective focus on the question of who ultimately makes decisions and controls participation in decision-making. The assumption is that power is exercised in a direct, observable conflict over issues recognized as relevant.

Power can also be used to prevent issues from being raised. Two-dimensional approaches to power investigate decisions, as well as non-decisions. A non-decision neutralizes or eliminates any latent or overt threat to the vested interests of the powerful. Non-decisions do not necessarily manifest themselves in overt behavior and do not only relate to recognized issues. The two-dimensional view of power focuses particularly on potential issues. This type of issue remains invisible as a result of non-decision-making. In this view, the exercise of power is not necessarily based on observable conflict, but may also ensue from covert, but in principle observable, conflict.

Lukes' three-dimensional view of power involves a thoroughgoing critique of the two previous views which, he feels, are too behavioral. He conceptualizes the different ways in which issues are kept out of an arena of conflict, whether through individual decisions, or through the operation of dominant values and institutional procedures. Genuine consensus does not necessarily exist because no grievances can be detected.

The third dimension Lukes adds is latent conflict, that is, a hidden discrepancy of interests of those exercising power and those subject to this power. The conflict is latent in the sense that it would arise if subordinates would express their needs and wishes. These unexpressed desires or preferences that would be expressed in a condition of relative autonomy by powerless groups or individuals are considered as real interests by Lukes.

According to Lukes, the attribution of an exercise of power involves the claim that A acts (or fails to act) in such a way that B does (or fails to do) what he or she would not do otherwise (the term 'do' includes 'think', 'feel' or 'want'). Specifically, Lukes offers two guidelines to the empirical identification of power. First, the relevant counterfactual has to be identified, that is, what B would have done (or failed to do) in the absence of A's power. In order to trace this counterfactual, we must explore those alternatives which are not realized. How would B react to a hypothetical or real opportunity to act differently from the way A had wanted him or her to? In the case of overt conflict, the relevant counterfactual is easily identified: if A and B are in conflict, A wanting x and B wanting y, then, if A prevails over B, we can assume that B would otherwise have done y. Where there is no overt conflict, we must provide other grounds for asserting that if A acts in a certain way, B would have acted differently from the way she or he did in reality. Secondly, Lukes advocates uncovering the mechanism which enabled A to exercise power. In looking for the power mechanism, it must be acknowledged, according to Lukes, that the exercise of power can be the result of inaction, that power may be exercised by collectives and institutions, and that A neither has to be aware of the actual reason or motive for his or her action, nor of the way in which B interprets A's action. If A is unable to perceive the effects his or her action has on B, it is not justified, Lukes argues, to speak of the exercise of power. There can only be an exercise of power if A is actually capable of not exercising power by acting differently. In Lukes' view, the assignment of power is at the same time the assigment of partial or full responsibility for certain consequences.[2]

Most criticisms of Lukes focus on the concept of real interests, arguing that it is evaluative, as Lukes pointed out himself in 1974. In view of this criticism, I decided in my own research not to attempt uncovering any real interests of married women and men. I rejected the notion of real interests mainly because of its association with the concept of false consciousness, and did not make any assumption about the relative truth of different layers in human consciousness. Nor did I try to determine empirically which part of the respondents' consciousness reflected their most genuine beliefs. Instead, I aimed at identifying subjective preferences under hypothetical conditions of autonomy, the conditions, according to Lukes, to detect relevant counterfactuals, that is, what someone would have done if no power had been exercised, or did not do because power was exercised. Furthermore, I attempted to uncover the power mechanisms which determine subjective preferences by looking for the hidden ideological forces which constitute women's and men's wishes concerning certain domains of their marriage.

One crucial problem, however, remained to be solved: how to distinguish empirically between consensus and pseudo-consensus? If people turn out to be incapable of imagining any desired alternatives to their present situation as a result of a general state of resignation and passivity, what evidence can be provided for the hypothesis that power is involved? Gramsci's work on ideological hegemony offered a solution to this problem.

Gramsci (1971) conceives of ideological hegemony as the result of a slow social process in which consensus is developed between dominant and subordinate groups. Consensus is expressed in the approval by subordinate groups of the dominant values, symbols, beliefs and opinions. Social institutions such as the educational system, religion, mass media etc., which serve to breed culture, contribute in significant ways to the evolution of a social consensus. Public opinion and the prevailing cultural climate make actions performed by subordinate groups appear to spring from their free will, whereas, in fact, they reflect a necessity resulting from existing relationships of dominance.

In Gramsci's notion of ideological hegemony, 'common sense' plays a crucial part. Hegemonic control is achieved by generating representations in common-sense thought in which social contradictions appear as unitary wholes. Control, however, is not total. This is reflected in the fact that the common-sense conception of the world is fragmentary, incoherent and often inconsistent. It is in the ambiguities and contradictions of common sense that the differentiation in the values of dominant and subordinate groups becomes visible. From this, the following three characteristics of ideological hegemony can be inferred (cf. van den Brink 1978):

1   the ideology is 'prevailing' because it has become part of everyday thought;
2   the ideology is 'organizing' in that it promotes social cohesion by representing contradictions as unitary;
3   'necessity' is represented as 'freedom'; in the ideology particular interests of dominant groups are experienced as general interests and, therefore, they can be freely accepted by subordinate groups.

In fact, these characteristics might serve as empirical criteria to detect 'breaches' of the general consensus with respect to gender relationships. If it were possible to trace these characteristics in common-sense thought and beliefs about women and men, this could tell us a great deal about the ideological underpinnings of power in gender relationships.

The central concern of my research on marital power was the quality of power, reflected in power processes and mechanisms rather than its quantity: the way the 'power pie' is divided up between married women and men. I was also interested in the ways in which power processes manifest themselves in different social practices and in the circumstances in which women and men live. Does social class make any difference? How is power related to women's being or not being employed? I defined power processes as taking place when one of the marriage partners desires certain changes which are either effected or thwarted in some way. Desired changes, as the expression of subjective preferences, were then regarded as the 'relevant counterfactuals'.

I distinguished five elements in power processes: desires for (or attempts at) change; structural or psychological impediments; the partner's reaction to change; strategies to realize or prevent change and conflicts that may arise in the process of change. My assumption was that the reasons and motivations for the presence or absence of desires for (or attempts at) change can both shed light on power processes and, in so doing, illuminate the reasons for the absence of conflict. Since power in marital relationships can be either overt or, more or less, covert, I made a theoretical distinction between manifest power, latent power and 'invisible power mechanisms'. Manifest power surfaces in attempts at change, strategies and conflicts. Latent power is present if the needs and wishes of the more powerful person are anticipated or if change is not attempted. In that case, conflict is avoided because of resignation due to the expected negative reaction from the partner or the fear of jeopardizing the marital relationship. Finally, 'invisible power mechanisms' are understood as social or psychological mechanisms, which do not necessarily surface in overt behavior, but may manifest themselves in systematic sex differences of mutual and self-esteem and in opinions about, or perceptions and legitimations of, everyday reality. The concept of 'invisible power mechanisms' indicates that both their operation and their effects generally escape awareness.

The data (see Komter 1989a for a more detailed

discussion) showed that manifest and latent ('anticipatory') power are characterizing marital relationships in manifold ways. For instance, women made more attempts at changing several domains of their marriage than their husbands, but they were less effective in realizing their wishes compared to men (manifest power). If women and men desired no change the women's attitudes showed more often resignation than men's who were more unequivocally satisfied (latent power). This became apparent from the different quality of the 'no-answers' of women and men to the question of whether they desired some changes in their marriage (Lukes' 'relevant counterfactual', see above). Finally, 'invisible power' showed up in the following ways: in systematic gender differences of self-esteem and esteem for the partner, men were more highly valued, both by their wives and by themselves; in perception of daily life, men systematically underestimated their wives' share in household tasks and responsibilities and overestimated their sexual needs, thereby demonstrating wishful thinking; in legitimations in which the often contradictory and ambiguous character of daily experience was represented as a unitary whole; for example, men had more positive feelings about household labor than women; however, in the legitimations, 'he dislikes it' or 'she likes it more' *were* frequently mentioned.

On the basis of the empirical results, Lukes' concept of three-dimensional power seemed most suited to uncovering manifest and latent power involving events and non-events as reflected in overt as well as covert grievances. Gramsci's notion of ideological hegemony was useful for detecting regularities in the inconsistencies and contradictions in the common-sense thought and daily experiences of married women and men.

The theoretical framework outlined above did make it possible to give an account of the nature of power processes in marital relationships and the way these are related to differences in social positions, such as social class and women's having or not having a paid job. Particularly, the subtle and often covert nature of marital power could be made visible by means of this theoretical approach.

Conclusion

In this chapter, I have presented two kinds of argument against the development of a general feminist theory of power and gender. First, I argued that the universalistic pretensions of such theorizing make it impossible to do justice to both the categorical and the particular characteristics of gender: the dual character of gender as displaying both structured regularity and diversity within the category of 'women' (or 'men'). Secondly, I argued that the differences between power in gender relations and in other types of power relations are less fundamental than the similarities between them. Power in gender relations does not seem to work in fundamentally different ways, nor to have fundamentally different consequences, in comparison to other social relations involving power. Power has no gender (although gender is tied to power).

Existing theoretical approaches to power, for example those offered by Lukes (1974) and Giddens (1979) (see Davis, this volume), might be profitably used in feminist analysis. They offer specific insights in specific areas of feminist concern. As long as one does not pretend to explain global categories like 'femininity' or 'gender' by means of the concept of power, but instead focus on specific instances in which gender and power are intertwined, the concept of power may be useful for feminist theorizing. It can illuminate the manifold and subtle interactional and ideological processes which are producing and reproducing sexual inequality.

Returning one last time to the story of feminism's love affairs, I would conclude that subjection to one marital partner for life does not seem to be a very promising strategy for feminism. A deliberate choice in favor of several and diverse partners, in conformity with the needs of the moment, is likely to be more healthy.

Notes

I am grateful to Kathy Davis for her valuable comments.
1 From her contribution to the symposium 'The Gender of Power' it appears that Hartsock has revised her earlier opinion on this matter; she now seems to endorse a more differentiated view (Hartsock 1987).
2 In a more recent publication (Lukes 1986), it appears that Lukes has revised his earlier views on the ways power is linked with interests, conflict and responsibility.

PART TWO

POWER, STRUCTURE AND AGENCY

3
Critical Sociology and Gender Relations
KATHY DAVIS

Within feminist scholarship, gender has occupied a privileged position as the central concept, undisputedly part and parcel of any study in the field. Based on their critique of traditional disciplines, feminists have formulated theoretical frameworks for analyzing social life using gender as focus and analytic tool, 'through which the division of social experience along gender lines tends to give men and women different conceptions of themselves, their activities and beliefs, and the world around them' (Harding 1986: 31).

Gender has been investigated in terms of the individual (how men and women behave, their beliefs and attitudes, gender identity), in terms of social structure (gendered divisions in the social activities or labor of men and women) and in terms of symbolic orders (gender symbolism, how we think about 'masculinity' and 'feminity'). At each of these levels, gender has not simply been regarded as a matter of difference between individuals or social organizations or human thought, but rather as a power asymmetry. In other words, whereas gender differences may – in and of themselves – be of some academic interest, for feminists the primary concern has been with how this difference constructs asymmetrical power relations between men and women – relations involving domination and subordination. Thus, it is at the moment that the issue of gender embraces the issue of power that it becomes of particular interest and relevance to feminists.

The issue of power has not fared nearly as well as gender within feminist scholarship, however. Originally, power was viewed as something that only men 'had'. Since we were going to devote ourselves to the position of women, we found ourselves focusing on oppression as the female experience *par excellence*. In our dealings with one another, power was an even less acceptable item. In fact, it was something of a dirty word, conjuring up images of competitive, career-oriented females, stepping over the backs of their less fortunate sisters or hob-nobbing with men for a piece of the pie. It obviously had no place in the egalitarian women's communities we envisioned for ourselves.

Times have changed. We soon discovered that even women's groups were not free of power; that women were different; and – to make matters worse – some of us were more powerful than others of us. Within feminist scholarship, power has since become a legitimate topic of study. Gender relations now tend to be automatically viewed as relations of power. Feminist scholars are increasingly concerning themselves with how these relations come to be constructed, maintained and, of course, undermined in the various areas of social life.

Having established that power and gender are inevitably connected and that this relation is of primary concern to feminists, including the scholars among us, the next question becomes: how can the relationship between gender and power best be theorized? There are basically two possibilities. In the first case, gender is taken as the central concept and an attempt is made to develop a specifically feminist theory on power and gender. This assumes that social experience, including relations of power between the sexes, can best be understood in terms of gender. It also assumes that power has indeed a gender, i.e. that there are specific forms of power operating in gender relations. And, finally, it assumes that a specifically feminist perspective on power is required.

In the second case, power is taken as the central concept and an attempt is made to elaborate traditional or critical theories on power within the social sciences to include relations between the sexes. This assumes that social experience, including gender relations, can best be understood in terms of power. It also assumes that power does not have a gender (although the two go hand-in-hand in practice). And, finally, it assumes that a feminist critique of existing theories of power is required in order to make them applicable to understanding how power works in gender relations.

In the context of a study on power and gender in medical encounters, I was faced with this choice as well (Davis 1988a,b). My research concerned how women's complaints were being defined, diagnosed and treated in consultations with male general practitioners and how asymmetrical relations of power are being produced, reproduced and undermined in the process. It was, in short, a micro-analysis of power in a specific institutionalized gender relationship.

It could have been tackled using either gender or power as theoretical focus. On the one hand, a theory of gender might have been employed in order to account for asymmetries between male physicians and female patients in medical interaction. On the other hand, a theory of power could have been selected from those available within the social sciences in order to analyze gender relations in the context of general practice consultations. In both cases, however, the theoretical framework would have had some missing pieces. Theories of gender do not deal with power explicitly; theories of power tend to be silent when it comes to the subject of gender. Thus, either way gaps would need to be filled in and adaptations made to meet the particular requirements of my own inquiry. Faced with this difficult choice, I ultimately opted for the latter route and turned to current (critical) social theory on power, in particular Giddens' (1976, 1979, 1984) theory of structuration, for help in delineating the workings of power in encounters between women and their doctors.

In this chapter, an attempt will be made to discuss some of the advantages and disadvantages of Giddens' theory for coming to terms with some of the problems which can emerge in the analysis of power and gender at the level of face-to-face interaction. After locating the theory of structuration within current debates about power in the social sciences and setting out some of its central features, an attempt will be made to demonstrate its merits for my own inquiry. Although I shall be showing why Giddens' theory of power proved a felicitous choice for my own study of power and gender in medical encounters, my conclusion will not be that I have, therefore, discovered the solution to the problems currently faced by feminist theory on gender and power. On the contrary, I shall be arguing that the entire question of choice – which theory is most adequate for investigating power relations between the sexes – is itself in need of revision. In conclusion, I shall be making some suggestions for a direction that feminist theorizing on power and gender might more profitably take.

Problems in theorizing power

Feminists are not the first (social) scientists to encounter difficulties in theorizing power. In fact, since the inception of sociology as a science, power has been rather standard fare for debate. Despite massive theorizing concerning the 'nature of the beast', however, there appears to be little agreement as to how it should be defined. As Lukes (1982), himself a leading theorist on power, notes: when it comes to power, one is left with the unavoidable impression that 'anything goes'.[1]

Whereas the last word has yet to be said on the subject of power, several attempts have been made to sort out some of the dilemmas involved in theorizing about it. According to Lukes (1979), there are primarily three bones of contention or 'contests', which regularly emerge in discussions about power.

Agency v. structural determinism

Should power be linked to human agency or is it a form of structural determinism? This question concerns the extent to which a person has some freedom of choice ('could have done otherwise'), even in asymmetrical power relations or whether individual activity can best be described as determined by socially structured systems of domination.

The nature of power

Whereas everyone seems to agree that power involves A exercising some control over B's activities, the exact nature of that control is open to debate. Does power have to involve an overt or observable manifestation or can it be covert or even latent? To what extent does it have to be 'against B's interests' and, indeed, can we reasonably talk about 'interests' at all? Is power essentially a straightforward exercise of control or is it more likely to be elusive, ambiguous, complex and subtle?

Consensus v. coercion

Theories on power have tended to focus on power as consensus or power as coercion, but not both. To what extent should power be viewed as an essential and desirable component of highly organized societies? Or should power be regarded primarily in terms of domination and authority? Which approach has the most to offer for understanding contemporary society?

If these are the kinds of issue which inevitably arise in

discussions about power, then it makes sense to look for theories which attempt to resolve them or, at least, take them a step in the right direction. I shall now take a look at one such theory: Giddens' theory of structuration and, in particular, his notions of power.

Giddens' conception of power

Giddens attempts to resolve some of the controversies involved in the debates about power by providing a critique of the classics (Weber, Durkheim, Marx) as well as the more recent contributions to social theory (Goffman, Habermas, Althusser, Foucault). In an attempt to uncover some of their inherent theoretical weaknesses, he also tries to salvage their respective merits. This admittedly eclectic approach led to the development of his own theory of structuration, a 'grand theory' which – as he modestly notes – is applicable to 'all the concrete processes of social life' (Giddens 1984: xviii).

Within this 'grand theory', power occupies a central role. It is not something which can be 'tacked on' to other more basic concepts as, for example, to functionalism, where power is secondary to 'norms' and 'values' or in Marxist theory where 'class interest' is central and power an appendage which will disappear miraculously along with class divisions. In his view, social theories which disregard the centrality of power in social life will inevitably prove to be inadequate.

Taking the position that power is central to the study of social life does not, however, mean that it automatically becomes more central than other concepts. He rejects the tendency of Foucault and company who, under the influence of a 'Nietzchean radicalization of power', give power primacy over everything else. Power appears as some kind of 'mysterious phenomenon, that hovers everywhere and underlies everything' (Giddens 1984:

226). The result is a reductionism every bit as faulty as functionalist and Marxist reductionisms were.

In his framework, Giddens treats power as one of several primary concepts, each essential for the analysis of social life. They are all clustered around relations involving action and structure and cannot be explicated without reference to this relationship. In this relationship, which Giddens calls 'duality of structure', social structure and human action do not stand in opposition, but rather presuppose one another: 'Structure [is] the medium and outcome of the conduct it recursively organizes; the structural properties of social systems do not exist outside of action but are chronically implicated in its production and reproduction' (Giddens 1984: 374).

Taking the 'duality of structure' as starting point, Giddens is able to conceptualize power in a way which is dynamic, processual and, at the same time, highly complex. It goes beyond the scope of this chapter to deal with Giddens' theory of structuration, including his notions on power, in any comprehensive way.[2] Instead, I shall limit myself to those dimensions of his concept of power which make it especially relevant to the study of power at the level of face-to-face interaction; that is, how actors draw upon rules and resources in order to influence the course of a conversation and, in the process, construct (asymmetrical) relations of power.

Giddens' conception of power has the following five dimensions:

1 *Power is integral to social interaction.*   Power is implicated at all levels of social life, from the level of 'global cultures and ideologies' all the way down to the 'most mundane levels of everyday interactions' (Giddens 1976: 113). The analysis of power is not limited to social institutions or political collectivities, but can also take a face-to-face encounter as its starting point. Any instance of social interaction involves three elements: its constitution as meaningful; its constitution as a moral or normative order;

and its constitution as the operation of relations of power. These elements are 'subtly, but tightly' interwoven, making it impossible to deal with one without taking the other into account (Giddens 1979: 104–113). Power involves the skills and resources which members bring to and mobilize in the production of interaction, thereby directing or influencing its course. It is implicated in the production of meaning in the sense that actors have capabilities for making certain 'accounts count'. It is also involved in ensuring compliance to moral claims. Members exercise power by enacting or resisting sanctions. Analyzing power entails showing how it is involved in both the production of meaning as well as the constitution and maintenance of normative orders concerning how the situation and the respective social position of the participants are to be defined.

2   *Power is intrinsic to human agency.*   There can be no study of power which does not take agency into account. In its most general sense, power is agency. It is the 'can' which mediates the desired or intended outcomes of social actors and the actual realization of these outcomes in their daily social practices. It is also the 'could have done otherwise' which is implicated in every situation, even the most restrictive and oppressive (Giddens 1976: 11). By linking power to agency, the possibility is rejected that social actors are ever completely governed by social forces. Even when they display outward compliance with the oppressive contingencies of their situations, the conclusion is not warranted that they have been 'driven irrestibly and uncomprehendingly by mechanical pressures' beyond their control (Giddens 1984: 15). Compliance is often the result of a decidedly rational assessment of the situation and the viable alternatives; it does not automatically entail agreement.

Whereas Giddens rejects the notion that individuals can ever be completely powerless, he does not go to the other extreme and argue that society is made under circumstances of their own choosing. Social action is always bounded by 'unacknowledged conditions' and 'unintended consequences' (Giddens 1984: 9–14); that is, by conditions lying outside the actors' self-understanding. The analysis of power entails uncovering the subtle mix of what actors do (and refrain from doing), what they achieve (and fail to achieve) and what they might have done (but did not do).

3 *Power is relational, involving relations of dependence and autonomy.* Giddens locates power in a relationship between actors, whereby it can be 'harnessed to actors' attempts to get others to comply with their wants' (Giddens 1976: 93). To this end, resources and skills are mobilized by actors to accomplish their respective goals or influence the course of events in a desired direction. Unfortunately, members do not have equal access to resources for effecting the outcome of the interaction. Resources are asymmetrically distributed in accordance with structures of domination.

Despite this asymmetry, however, power relations are always reciprocal, involving some degree of autonomy and dependence in both directions. Power is never a simple matter of 'haves' and 'have nots'. Such a conception can only lead to an overestimation of the power of the powerful, closing our eyes to both the chinks in the armor of the powerful as well as the myriad ways that the less powerful have to exercise control over their lives, even in situations where stable, institutionalized power relations are in operation. Investigating power will therefore also involve uncovering the 'dialectic of control': 'how the less powerful manage resources in such a way as to exert control over the more powerful in established power relationships' (Giddens 1984: 374).

4 *Power is enabling as well as constraining.* In many of the contexts of everyday life, power does go hand-in-hand with structured forms of domination. Actors do not simply intervene in the course of events, but they also try to exercise control over one another. This is accomplished by means of sanctions which are structurally available. By means of sanctioning processes, some actors can restrict

the activities of other actors or get them to do things that they might not normally have done under other circumstances. Whereas this sanctioning can be accomplished by means of threat, force or violence, this is the exception. More common or mundane sanctions entail disapproval, criticism or simply an absence of response (Giddens 1984: 175).

Sanctions are not only restrictive, however. They can be enabling as well, inducing actors to engage in specific activities. In fact, sanctions are the very means by which social interaction comes to be constituted as orderly and 'normal'. This means that power cannot be equated with forms of domination despite their 'inherent social association'; nor is power an 'inherently noxious phenomenon'. A person always retains the 'capacity to say no' (Giddens 1984: 32). Power is also involved in the very constitution of social life, making it productive, enabling and even positive.

Any analysis of power, then, will entail sorting out both dimensions and showing how power is connected to constraint and enablement in specific instances of social interaction.

5 *Power is processual.* Power is exercised as a process, part and parcel of the perpetual flux of situated practices of social actors. Structured relations of power involving domination and subordination are produced and reproduced through these practices. Just as members routinely and continually construct the 'normal appearances' of their everyday lives, they will simultaneously, and in similar ways, be constructing power relations. Power will be exercised as members reflexively monitor their interaction and employ skills and resources in flexible, on-the-spot and, above all, habitual ways in order to gain control over the encounter. This conception of power does not focus on the outcome or product of power or who has 'more' of it, but rather on the 'hows' of power. In other words, the focus is on how actors routinely construct, maintain, but also change and transform their relations of power.

In conclusion, Giddens' conception of power is suited to a micro-analysis of power. It does not treat power as straight-forward, top-down or repressive. Far from being a matter of openly authoritarian forms of control, power can also be enabling or productive. It has a Janus-face. Power is regarded as mundane, processual and multidimensional, whereby relations of power involving domination and subordination are constructed in the course of interaction by means of the same reflexive procedures employed by actors to structure or sustain any situation.

Having briefly described Giddens' conception of power, particularly as it can be applied to the analysis of face-to-face interaction, I shall return to the question posed at the beginning of this chapter. What does Giddens' view of power have to offer specifically for an inquiry like mine into how power works in medical interaction and, more generally, for feminist theorizing on the relationship between gender and power?

Conceptualizing power in interaction between the sexes

At the outset of my inquiry into medical consultations between female patients and male GPs, I expected to find the kinds of phenomena so abundantly and convincingly described in feminist literature on women and health care: physicians undermining women's control and authority over their reproduction (Arms 1975; Culpepper 1978; Ehrenreich and English 1979; Oakley 1979; Fisher 1986; Martin 1987), making moralistic statements about women's roles as wives and mothers or about their sexuality (Scully and Bart 1973; Lorber 1976; Fidell 1980; Scully 1980; Standing 1980; Fisher and Groce 1985), not taking their complaints seriously (Homans 1985; MacPherson 1988), finding psychological disorder in even the most harmless complaint (Lenanne and Lenanne 1973; Davis 1986), prescribing tranquilizers at the drop of a hat (Cooperstock 1978) and so on.

Much to my surprise (and, admittedly, chagrin),[3] I was forced to conclude, having listened to numerous taped consultations, that the GPs were behaving in an undisputedly friendly and benevolent fashion. They displayed an unflaggingly sympathetic interest in their patients' problems, even the most trivial ones. They had obviously received social skills training and were familiar with the more holistic approaches to medicine. Whereas they did prescribe tranquilizers for their female patients, it was only with great hesitancy and reluctance. In fact, it was almost as though I had wandered into a conversation between two friends rather than an institutional encounter. It did not look anything like a power struggle.

Just as I had expected the doctors of my study to display the behavior of the powerful, authoritatively wielding the sceptre of control throughout the consultations, I was prepared to discover the patients scarcely able to hold their own, hapless and helpless in the face of the combined forces of institutional authority and male domination. Whereas it was undoubtedly true that the patients did not, when all was said and done, come out on top in the interactional power struggles, I could not help but notice that they were not going down without a fight. It was abundantly clear that, just as male doctors could be nice and friendly while exercising control, patients were often surprisingly recalcitrant and rebellious. In fact, the patients routinely exercised power in all sorts of subtle, sneaky and even somewhat unorthodox ways. Although the consultations were conducted in a cooperative and – as previously mentioned – friendly fashion, patients could engage in activities that served to undermine the physician's authority over their problems as well as what was to be done about them. These power practices were not dramatic, but rather microscopic attempts to shift the power imbalance in favor of the patient.

Even my initial confrontation with my data convinced me that power was not going to be an easy thing to come to terms with. This conviction was fuelled, however, by my experience with feminist literature on interaction between the sexes. Whereas power had become an undeniable topic within these studies, it was often conceptualized in a way which was problematic. Originally, studies on interaction were not about power and gender at all.[4]

Social interaction tended to be viewed as an essentially orderly and harmonious enterprise – a cooperative coproduction involving the activities of all participants (Garfinkel 1967). These participants, otherwise referred to as 'members', had, in principle at least, access to the same kinds of interactional resources for engaging in social interaction. In other words, they were peers in the interaction game. Apparently, they did not have a gender. Feminist scholars have since taken issue with this stance. They specifically examined interaction between men and women in a variety of social contexts: private conversations between couples and mixed groups (Henley 1977; Fishman 1978), the public arena of television talkshows and meetings (Trömel-Plötz 1984), and institutional settings like medical consultations, the courtroom and the classroom (Fisher and Todd 1983, 1986). What they discovered, quite simply, was that where gender was a part of the interaction, power was soon to follow. An explicit attempt was made to uncover how the asymmetrical power relations between men and women were being constructed within and through their talk.

In most cases, this was accomplished by studying the sequential organization of the conversations and showing how women and men do not have equal access to the interactional resources for ordering that talk. The findings are of no great surprise. It would seem that men have a tendency to hog the conversational floor. They get their topics initiated and talked about more often, interrupt with equanimity and are notably reticent about performing the 'interactional shit-work' (Fishman 1978) which is necessary for any conversation, if it is to proceed in a pleasant and well-oiled fashion. Just as unsurprisingly, women seem to have considerable difficulty getting the floor. Once they do, their topics tend to get broken off midstream or are taken over by others. They are subject to constant interruption and are rarely the recipients of 'interactional shit-work', but rather the ones who do it. It is my contention that these studies have primarily two things to tell us about gender and power in face-to-face interaction. First, conversational power is something that men have and women do not. Secondly, power relations between the sexes in conversational contexts have as their most distinguishing feature control, restraint and repression. In other words, the model of power and gender relations being employed in feminist studies on interaction is a top-down, repressive one.

At this point, the reader, particularly if she is a feminist, might be inclined to ask: 'So what's wrong with that?' In fact, this model of power and gender relations does bear considerable resemblance to our interactional experiences as women. Or, as Trömel-Plötz (1984) rather pessimistically notes, this is women's 'conversational lot in life'. Moreover, it is a model which has stood us in good stead as we have attempted to uncover the inequities faced by women in the various contexts of their everyday lives.

While I do not believe that this model is entirely wrong, it clearly had some rather serious drawbacks as a conceptual framework for understanding the workings of power in my own research. How was I to come to terms with my friendly doctors and resistant patients? Moreover, it is a model which is of limited usefulness in understanding gender and power more generally. The main problem is that it draws implicitly upon what I shall refer to as feminist 'common-sense' notions on gender relations.[5] Despite the merits of these notions, they are not infallible

Advice Centre Availability

Drop-in	When	Where
City Campus You can drop in for initial enquiries during opening times	Appointments only Mon, Tues, Wed & Fri: 10am-4pm Thurs: 12 noon-4pm	Advice Centre, The HUBS
Collegiate Campus	Mon, Weds & Fri 10am - 3pm	Advice Centre, 202 Oaklands Building

Student Union Advice Centre

City Campus: Advice Centre, The HUBS, Sheffield, S1 1WB

Collegiate Campus: 202 Oaklands Building, Sheffield, S10 2BP

Telephone: 0114 225 4148

Contact form: http://go.shu.ac.uk/advice

 @SHSU_Advice

Advice Centre
Signposting

Hallam Help

Enquiry			
Housing	☐	State Benefits	☐
Student Loan	☐	Academic	☐
Financial Hardship	☐	Student Complaints	☑
Hate Crime reporting	☐	Other (please specify)	
Signposted by *Sara D*		....	

You can attend the Advice Centre to speak to a staff member about your issue. If it is a complex issue, they may ask you to book an appointment. You can contact them in person, by phone or via contact form https://go.shu.ac.uk/advice

and, in fact, are in need of some elaboration. It is to this issue that I shall now direct my attention.

Feminist common sense on power

Feminist 'common sense', both traditionally and in the present, tends to treat power within gender relations as basically top-down and repressive. Women are regarded as the inevitable victims of male supremacy, helpless and hapless at the hands of the evil-intentioned, omnipotent male. Power, by the same token, is automatically linked to relations involving domination and authoritarian forms of control or coercion, making it difficult to see it as anything but negative and repressive. This view of power has methodological and political implications for investigating interaction between men and women.

I shall begin with the notion that power between the sexes can best be viewed as top-down. One of the main contributions of conversation analysis and, more generally, ethnomethodology and the 'interpretative sociologies' was to break radically with mainstream Parsonian sociology and its treatment of the individual as 'cultural dope', blindly driven by social forces beyond her control. A valiant attempt was made to retrieve the social actor as basically competent and knowledgeable. Studies in the field were, in fact, devoted to displaying just how – often surprisingly – capable members were at finding their way about in social life. Social interaction was always and everywhere viewed as a human accomplishment, actively and knowledgeably negotiated by the participants themselves.

This stance of uncovering how ordinary people 'do social life' and giving them at least a little credit for knowing what was going on is one of the initial attractions of conversation analysis as research orientation. It is a stance, however, which seems to disappear as soon as the participants turn out to have a gender. In that case, it is suddenly the man who does the interacting, negotiating the encounter all by himself, while the woman sits passively and helplessly on the sidelines, at best the respondent to his activities. Unwittingly, perhaps, it would seem that as soon as gender enters the interactional scene, women are transformed into that 'cultural dope' we used to be so interested in avoiding. This is more than a methodological inconsistency, however. It has political implications as well.

It goes almost without saying that feminist scholars have always been especially interested in how women fare in the various contexts of their daily lives. Whereas the original concern was with domination or 'systems of male control and coercion', there has been a growing emphasis in recent years on how women themselves 'participate in setting up, maintaining, and altering the system of gender relations' (Gerson and Peiss 1985: 322). The idea is not to deny the fact that structured asymmetries exist in the resources available to men and women for exercising control over what happens in any encounter, nor to blame women for their own oppression. It is, however, important to delineate how relations of power are being negotiated; that is, the process by which relations involving domination and subordination are produced, reproduced and transformed. This requires, among other things, being particularly alert to how women exercise control, even when their resources are limited, or when they do not, when all is said and done, come out on top. It also involves directing our attention at the often microscopic and sometimes even trivial ways in which women routinely undermine asymmetrical power relations or display some degree of penetration of what is going on, despite being unable or unwilling at that particular moment to do anything to alter the course of events.

It is this concern with the 'boundaries' – how women and men delineate their relations at any given time or place – that is essential for coming to terms with processes of change. Uncovering how they 'make and reshape their social worlds' (Gerson and Peiss 1985: 321) enables us, ultimately, to explain how and why these boundaries change or, more to the point, might be changed at some future date. In short, an adequate feminist analysis of gender relations requires replacing a top-down model of power with a model which treats power relations as something to be negotiated by parties who both have access to some resources, albeit unequal ones.

The second notion inherent in feminist common sense concerning power in gender relations is that power is inevitably linked to domination and subordination. The implication of this linkage is that power is basically a nasty business, employed by men for the sole purpose of keeping women down, silencing them or otherwise preventing them from acting, thinking or feeling as they would choose to do, when left to their own devices. There are several difficulties with such a conception of power.

First, if we want to investigate power we will be forced to look for it in situations which involve overt and authoritarian forms of control by men over women. This eliminates those instances of interaction between the sexes which are friendly, pleasant or intimate. Since much of the interaction between men and women could be characterized in precisely this way, including my own research, a model of power is clearly required which will enable us to investigate it anywhere. In other words, we need a model of power relations which can also deal with power as it is exercised in friendly or intimate encounters.

Secondly, if power relations are strictly of the coercive or repressive kind, it is difficult to account for why women continue to go along with them. The only possible explanation becomes that they are, indeed, powerless to do anything about them or, more probably, the misguided victims of what used to be dubbed 'false consciousness'. This, once again, relegates women squarely to the position of 'cultural dope', that passive and unenlightened victim of circumstances beyond her control.

Thirdly, if power is equated with domination and sub-ordination, it is difficult to see how we as feminists could ever develop forms of social action and interaction which are something different from that. What would our feminist alternative be? We can criticize, but we are unable to come up with anything better. In other words, we are forced into a kind of political nihilism. An adequate feminist model of power will need to take into account that power is not only linked to domination, but can also be a potentially positive or enabling force.[6] In conclusion, whereas 'feminist common sense' is an essential pre-requisite for examining power in gender relations, it is neither complex nor dynamic enough to come to terms with many of the everyday encounters between the sexes.

Theorizing power and gender

In order to come to terms with how power works to construct asymmetrical gender relations at the level of face-to-face interaction, a conception of power is needed which enables us to link agency to structured relations involving domination and subordination. We need to be able to reinstate women to the position of agency without falling into the concomitant stance of blaming them for social inequities. And, we have to come to terms with the Janus-face of power, uncovering the subtle and multi-faceted complexities of its workings in many everyday encounters between the sexes. As we have seen, Giddens' theory of structuration deals with precisely these issues, making it a useful starting point for coming to terms with power in interaction between the sexes. Before closing this chapter with an unqualified endorsement of his theory, however, a few words of caution are in order.

Giddens, like most social theorists of power, does not address the subject of gender, gender relations or power relations between the sexes.[7] In fact, both his theory of structuration as well as his conception of power are completely devoid of any connection with concrete contexts or the situated practices of social actors. His theory is general and highly abstract, making it, at best, a heuristic framework for the enterprising investigator brave enough to try to use it.

Power is, of course, always and everywhere contextual. It entails a relationship between specific actors or groups, drawing upon specific rules and resources, organized in specifically structured ways. Power cannot be analyzed without reference to sex, class, region, historical period or whatever. As Thompson notes:

> what is at issue is the fact that the restrictions on opportunities operate differentially, affecting unevenly various groups of individuals whose categorization depends on certain assumptions about social structure; and it is this differential operation or effect which cannot be grasped by the analysis of rules alone. (Thompson 1984: 159)

This means that Giddens' notions of power, as well as his theory of structuration as a whole, are urgently in need of both empirical and theoretical grounding. When this is done – as I have attempted in my own research on medical encounters (Davis 1988a, b) – the result is a grounded theory of gender relations as power relations in a specific social context. Using both structural and individual approaches to power, it becomes possible to show how power works without losing women as subjects. Their contributions in producing, sustaining, but also under-mining and transforming relations involving domination and subordination can be uncovered without having to blame them for structured inequities. We can see power as something which is complex and subtle enough to account for much of the routine interaction between the sexes where straightforward forms of repression are not the order of the day.

In conclusion, an attempt has been made to show how it is possible to use a theory of power, taken from the (critical) sociological tradition, and apply it to the analysis of gender relations in a specific context. Whereas it enabled me to tackle certain theoretical problems which I had encountered within feminist scholarship in my own particular field of inquiry, it did so in abstract. The business of supplying the empirical grounding – showing how power worked in face-to-face interaction between women and men in medical settings – was left entirely to me. My choice for a suitable theoretical framework for analyzing gender and power was made on the basis of theoretical and empirical problems which arose in the course of my inquiry.

It is my contention that this is exactly how it should be. The question of which theoretical approach is best for the study of gender and power is itself a faulty one. It presupposes that there is a theory (or that one could be developed) which could, in principle, be used to account for gender and power at all levels of social life. It is this pretension which is in need of revision. The question is not whether we need a specific theory to explain how power is gendered. Neither is the issue whether or not we should re-enter the sociological mainstream in search of that one glorious theory which can be revised to meet our feminist ends. The relationship between gender and power is a complicated one; that much is clear. We need theories to help us to analyze asymmetrical relations involving power and gender in all areas and at all levels of social life. Considering the dazzling variety and complexity of social life, it seems highly improbable that any one theory – regardless of whether its starting point is gender or power – can ever hope to explain it all.

Instead of putting our efforts into the zealous pursuit of the 'perfect theory', I would suggest that we should move in the other direction. We need theories which are, above all, anchored in our experiences – as women, as feminists, but also as scholars grappling with specific questions about power and gender, applied to specific settings and analyzed with specific research methods. Taking these experiences as starting point, we must develop theories which will help us come to terms with the concrete social practices of the women and men in the contexts we are investigating. Moreover, they must be based on a sophisticated and reflective feminist critique of how asymmetrical gender relations are being constructed, maintained and undermined in those specific contexts. It is my contention that one theoretical perspective on gender and power – a kind of feminist 'grand theory' – is not what we need. We need feminist theory on gender and power which is grounded.

Notes

1 For example, power is something which is possessed; it can only be exercised; it is a matter of authority. Power belongs to the individual; it belongs only to collectivities; power doesn't belong to anyone, but is a feature of social relations. Power usually involves conflict, but it doesn't have to. Power presupposes resistance; power is primarily involved in compliance (to norms); power is both. Power is tied to repression and domination; power is productive and enabling. Power is bad, good, demonic or routine (Lukes 1982).

2 For a more complete discussion of how the theory of structuration can be applied to the study of power and gender, particularly in institutional settings, the reader is referred to Davis (1988b).

3 It was a project carried out explicitly under the banner of women's studies.

4 While there is also a variety of linguistic approaches to the study of language and interaction, my focus here will be on the sociological tradition of conversation analysis and ethnomethodology. Studies within this tradition have been concerned with how ordinary people engage in social practices using talk as a medium. For a good discussion of this approach, see Garfinkel (1967), Sacks et al. (1974) and, more recently, Atkinson and Heritage (1983).

5 The Schutzian notion of 'common sense' refers to mundane

understandings of social life or what people need to know in order to make sense of what they or others are doing in the course of their everyday lives. Obviously, for feminists, part of this 'common sense' will concern our (and other women's) experience with oppression and exploitation in social life. This experience as well as our beliefs about it form the basis of what I am calling feminist 'common sense' here. See also Stanley and Wise (1983).

6 This point has been made by Hartsock (1983) who argues that female theorists on power have always emphasized the positive aspects of power: 'power to' rather than 'power over'. A feminist perspective on power would need to include this along with an analysis of how relations involving domination and subordination are produced and reproduced between the sexes.

7 With the exception of the occasional gratuitous reference to the 'importance' of feminism as contemporary social movement or the 'desirability' of avoiding sexist pronoun usage in scientific texts (Giddens in Munters et al. 1935) – a bit scanty for someone who claims to have produced a 'grand theory' for explicating 'all the concrete processes of social life'.

4
Engendered Structure: Giddens and the Conceptualization of Gender

JOAN WOLFFENSPERGER

University education teaches students skills for managing and generating scientific knowledge. Learning the rules is not only a matter of discursive knowledge; practical consciousness is involved as well. Students are taught 'how to go on' in science. Gender-biased assumptions on the organization of society and on the nature of social science and self are an integral part of this process. Women's studies originated in the wake of the critique of the fundamentally gendered character of the social sciences.

In order to prevent the eventual production of gender differences and reproduction of gender inequality, feminist university teachers should be aware of gender organizing principles within academia. If university education is in some way or another structured according to gender, the credibility of women's studies education is at stake; an unintended consequence of their teaching practices can be the reproduction of male dominance.

While scientific research practices and methods have been problematized in women's studies, university education has received less attention. Recent research has, however, revealed several gender differences among university students in The Netherlands. Female participation is still lower, and female and male students are unequally distributed among the disciplines. Until recently, fewer women than men completed their studies. These phenomena have not been explained satisfactorily. Too often the focus is one-sidedly on female students, their 'role conflicts', their 'double-life perspective' (motherhood and job) and their lack of expectations and identification models (Derriks 1983; Saharso and Westerbeek 1983; Verwayen-Leijh 1985). Educational practices, or the organizing principles of the university system which create structured asymmetries between women and men, are not mentioned. Male students or teachers are also kept offstage, so that power and dominance stay hidden. Noticeably absent are questions of who is actually responsible for making rules in university education or of unequal access to resources. No attention is paid to the context of interaction. This model not only suffers from explanatory shortcomings, it is also politically wanting, facilitating a 'blame the victim' type of thinking.

Since the university system has been studied thoroughly in relation to gender differences, we might expect information on gender and university education to emerge. However, these studies remain limited in explanatory power because they tend to concentrate on only one side of the problem: either the individual actor's gendered qualities or the determining influence of the system on gender are analyzed.

In this chapter I will offer a theoretical perspective as a prerequisite for analyzing the relationship between gender and university education. The central question is: how should an alliance between gender and social system be conceptualized and is such an association to be expected in university education? In order to answer this question, a system's potentially gendered character, as well as how it systematically produces gender differences, needs to be analyzed comprehensively. A shift in focus must be made from women and men to gender differences themselves. Do they have a systematic character? How are they produced and reproduced? How are they related to power and domination?

A promising theoretical framework can be found in Anthony Giddens' theory of structuration. Although his awareness of gender (and ethnicity) is limited, his theory has several advantages for understanding gender differences in education. Since Giddens' theory is relatively unknown among feminist scholars, I shall describe it in some detail. I shall then introduce two new concepts – 'engendered structure' and 'twofold reproduction' – in order to articulate the relationship between gender differences and social systems. I shall screen the explanations already available on gender, education and university in the light of this theoretical framework, in order to assess the theoretical and political advantages for women's studies of a model in which agency, structure and gender are inextricably bound to each other.

Anthony Giddens' theory of structuration

Giddens has developed his social theory in reaction to postwar mainstream sociology. He has criticized interpretative traditions and philosophy of action (1976), functionalism (1976, 1979), and French structuralism (1979, 1984). Philosophers like Wittgenstein and Gadamer, as well as theoreticians like Marx, Habermas and Foucault, make their appearance as Giddens elaborates his own perspective on social reality. Methodological questions have his unceasing interest. He does not accept the traditional split in social theory: the subject–object dualism. He rejects the mutual exclusiveness of theorizing about either action or institutions. In the former case, purposefulness and accountability of action are thought to produce social reality. Power and the analysis of institutional features are lacking. Even the concept of action itself is deficient. In the latter case, human activities seem to be determined by factors which work behind people's backs. Here, human agents appear as zombies.

Giddens' theoretical efforts have a double target: to develop a more satisfactory theory of action and to transgress subject–object dualism via a refined conception of structure. In his theory of action, agency is based on two fundamental human qualities: capability and knowledge-ability. Agents are capable; they are able 'to act otherwise', thereby breaking routines. Action logically involves power in the sense of transformative capacity. Agents are also knowledgeable about the conditions of their daily activities, knowing 'how to go on' in a practical sense. They maintain a continuous 'theoretical' consciousness about the principles organizing their conduct. Every human being in fact is a practicing sociologist.

These assumptions on agency represent a political stance, which informs the rest of the theory on structuration. Knowledgeability and capability as innate qualities of human beings, whether women or men, seem to be justifiable starting points for any feminist theoretical model as well as feminist methods and methodology.[1]

To bridge the gap between subject and object and to transcend the dualism of voluntarism versus determinism, Giddens emphasizes the essentially recursive character of social life. He calls this recursiveness the *duality principle*. Agency and structure are not opposed to each other. At a logical level, they are necessarily connected. Action presupposes a notion of structure and vice versa.

Following de Saussure, Giddens develops a new conception of structure. Structure should be understood as '*présences*' and '*absences*'; it has no fixed form. It only 'exists' at the moment it is employed in interaction. Structure operates as a part–whole relationship; it cannot be perceived in its totality in concrete situations. It should be understood as means and outcome of social action and manifests itself as rules and resources, which can be thought of as system properties. Within a specific social system, rules and resources organize activities and, when mobilized in interaction, reproduce the system itself. In relation to this concept of structure, the concept of system is given a new meaning. A social system is the patterning of social relations across time and space, understood as reproduced practices.

Structure and system belong to an abstract order or mode of thinking, characterized by three closely related structural principles: domination, signification and legitimation. In social practices (reproduced relationships of autonomy and dependence) these principles are present as resources, interpretative schemes and norms. Using their practical knowledge of the situation, actors draw on rules and resources, and in doing so they produce activities and reproduce social systems. This conception of structure has important methodological implications. Embedded in the duality principle is the idea that agency produces institutions (practices, deeply ingrained in time and space) to the extent that these institutions are involved in the production of a specific social activity. Within the framework of the theory, the notion of recursiveness enables us to make analyses at two theoretical levels: the level of conduct and the level of institutions. At the level of conduct social activities can be studied and analyses can be made of how rules and resources are employed through practical and discursive consciousness. Rules (interpretative schemes and norms) can be understood as stocks of knowledge about communication and sanctions. Access to resources is related to power. In institutional analyses, the focus is on system properties. Here, rules and resources can be observed as media of system reproduction. Although conduct has been bracketed at this level, it should not be forgotten that systems only 'exist' as long as actors make use of system properties. The two levels of analysis are connected by the dual character of structure.

The same dualism, which motivated Giddens to develop his conception of duality of structure, can also be found in women's studies. Both voluntaristic theories, in which power and the constraining impact of structures of (male) domination are neglected, and deterministic approaches, which pay no attention whatsoever to women's know-ledgeability about their situation and their capability of breaking rules and routines, should be subjected to reflection and criticism. For feminist theory, Giddens' concept of structure opens up new avenues: gender can be analyzed in concrete situations and as domination, using the same conceptual framework. Pitfalls of voluntarism and of determinism can be avoided because system constraints and agents' capability are seen as inextricably linked. Strategies for structural change, aimed at under-mining male domination as an organizing principle, require an adequate analysis of gender in terms of system properties. A conceptualization of the relationship between structure and gender using Giddens' model seems both theoretically and politically interesting.

Patterns of gender difference

In his books, Giddens is rather silent on gender. Although he recognizes gender as a fundamental organizing principle and male domination as a fact, even where he is elaborating the concept of power, he makes no allusion to gender. This raises several questions: if gender is a basic organizing principle and if gender relations are to be characterized in terms of domination, then how is the relationship between gender and structure to be perceived? I brought this point up when I had the opportunity to interview Giddens. Although he confirmed the centrality of gender and ethnicity as organizing principles, he was 'not inclined to connect gender directly to the concept of structural principles' (Wolffensperger in Munters et al. 1985: 120). No arguments were given, however. In spite of Giddens' scepticism, I have since kept the idea of combining gender, as a central concept in feminist theorizing, and structure, as a central concept in the theory of structuration in mind.

What if a new concept of *engendered structure* could be introduced? Such a concept would have all the advantages of the structuration theory. It would place gender at the very heart of the model, exactly in the place where it belongs. Such a concept would refer to domination, signification and legitimation as gender organizing principles, as 'absences' structuring gender relations; and also to social practices in which these principles appear as *'présences'*, as rules and resources employed by agents.

If a specific social system has a gendered character, the searchlight in institutional analysis is turned to gendered system properties, organizing social practices according to gendered rules and resources. Gendered rules and resources should be conceived as media of a *twofold reproduction*. When employed in interaction, gender and social system are reproduced together; organized social differences between women and men are an integral part of social practices. It is only at the moment in which actors draw on gendered system properties that they reproduce the system involved as well as gender or gender relations. Thus, at the level of institutional analysis, gendered rules and resources must be studied not only as media of system reproduction, but as media of gender reproduction as well.

In order to test the usefulness of the twin concepts of engendered structure and twofold reproduction, I will take a look at the differences between women and men, both within the school system and the university. Do these differences have a gendered character? Are they institutionalized, and embedded in time and space?

Dutch statistics on gender and education show two types of patterning. Girls and boys are found in different places within the educational system; they follow different routes after primary school. Another gender pattern can be found in levels of education: the higher the level, the more the proportion of girls lags behind. Fewer girls than boys take advantage of their qualifications and enroll in the highest levels of schooling available in The Netherlands (Derde nota onderwijsemancipatie 1983; Oudijk 1983). In primary education, hardly any differences are found in attributes and results. In secondary school, however, differences in the performance of girls and boys in languages and mathematics/physics increase with age. Thus the low numbers of female students enrolling in the natural and technical sciences is not completely surprising. Within mainstream and vocational education, girls are distributed differently from boys.

Within the university system, there are also considerable differences among staff members. In The Netherlands, few female scientists are found in academia: only 15 per cent of the staff are female. They are over-represented in certain fields and under-represented in others. Moreover, in lower ranks, their proportion is relatively high and, in higher ranks, very low. Other differences are found in the sphere of personal life: female university staff members are less often married than their male colleagues. Though patterning among the disciplines is not identical in other countries, gender differences in horizontal and in vertical distribution are a general feature of universities (van Doorne-Huiskes 1983, 1986; Stolte-Heiskanen 1983; Hawkins and van Balen 1984).

A comparison of gender differences in the school and university systems shows interesting analogies. A gender-specific horizontal and vertical distribution can be found in both systems. Both types of distribution are related to a gender-based division of labor. In situated contexts, a gendered horizontal distribution creates minority positions. Girls or boys will, in certain types of schools and classes, be in a minority situation compared to pupils of the other sex. Within the university female staff members nearly always find themselves easily outnumbered by male colleagues. Gendered vertical dispersion is directly related to structures of (male) domination. Leaving the educational system earlier than boys, girls will enter the labor market at a lower level. Many working women have male bosses – both outside and inside academia. In accordance with their positions, the latter will also have better access to resources than their female employees.

Horizontal and vertical distributions can be seen as gendered properties of both the school and the university systems. They are the media of gender reproduction. The picture, however is not yet complete. More information is needed on how gendered system properties such as horizontal and vertical distributions are, in fact, related to school and university rules and resources. How differences are produced in interaction, in both the school and the university system.

Individual conduct

Several general studies have been carried out in The Netherlands, in which findings on gender in education and academia are summarized (Dekkers and Smeets 1982; Jungbluth and Schotel-Kraetzer 1982; Veeken 1982; Verwayen-Leijh 1985; van Eck and Veeken 1986; Koenders and Wolffensperger 1986). At the methodological level of interaction a 'personal characteristics' model turns out to be the only one available to explain gender differences. Several types of characteristics can be distinguished: biologically originated ones and socially constructed ones.

In the field of education, biology in its purest sense is used as an explanation. Although biology may have its (physical) impact, it should be approached with great scepticism when it comes to gender differences in conduct.[2] Biology cannot account for different performances according to gender in the field of mathematics and science, which increase with age. However, research on gender and mathematics still turns to biology for the answer. The notion of 'marriage-as-destiny' has been brought forward instead. Differences in patterns of distribution – and especially in vertical mobility – among female and male university staff are often explained in terms of marriage and the family. Marriage is considered to be some kind of biologically based female fate, which in itself is incompatible with an academic career; it is supposed seriously to hamper scientific productivity. As a result, female academics are said to lack vertical mobility. Unfortunately, destiny is no more convincing an explanation than is biology itself. Apart from the fact that many female scientists have never been married, and still do not reach the higher ranks, research has shown a very limited influence of marriage and/or children on productivity (Cole and Zuckerman 1987).

Differences in behavior and achievements are often explained as a result of individual decisions. Being socialized according to biological sex, the activities of female pupils and university staff tend to be gender-based. A process of self-selection takes place. Girls themselves prefer to leave school at an earlier age than boys, take different subjects and do not enroll in the highest levels of schooling available (Jungbluth and Schotel-Kraetzer 1982; Veeken 1982). If only girls would change their behavior! Female academics are also supposed to make gender-stereotyped decisions. Women choose certain disciplines and fields, part-time jobs, teaching instead of research, combining marriage with a university career (Bernard 1964; Cole 1979). If only women would act otherwise! However, research findings show unequivocally that in cases where both women and men have equal qualifications, female scientists are not likely to be appointed. Only if they possess excellent qualifications, their chances improve. Fewer women are found in on-line or top positions; those present earn lower wages for equal jobs. Productivity and publications being equal, a woman's upward mobility is slower. Funds and formal networks are less accessible to them. Even if they reach the top, they are excluded from informal contacts (Fidell 1970; Blackstone and Fulton 1975; Reskin 1978; Martin and Irvine 1982; van Doorne Huiskes 1986).

Let us take a closer look at the shortcomings of these theories based on female biology and destiny, and on female self-selection. Biological sex as well as processes of socialization according to biological sex tend to assume a determining character in the production of female identity and the organization of female activities. The model has no room for the ability to act otherwise. Female identity on one hand and female destiny on the other seem to determine activities, and to confine women to resignation and passivity. The model itself seems to promote observations on, and descriptions of, female agents in terms of socially approved gender stereotypes, and to produce 'femininity'. In the meantime, the self-selection perspective is often used, paradoxically, to point out women's own responsibility for patterned gender differences and related phenomena, like a gender-based division of labor, and the reproduction of gender asymmetery.

A flawed conception of agency, however, is not the only imperfection. Interestingly, in debates in which biology or individual decision-making is used as a justification for either change or continuation of existing inequalities, it is always *female* nature, destiny or choice which is studied. Male actors are hardly ever mentioned. Men, and their qualities, abilities and activities seem, self-evidently, to be the standard. Assumptions on biological differences and 'male normalcy' seem to go hand in hand, the organizing principles of legitimation and of signification seem to be connected to biological differences. Just as problematic is the complete lack of contextuality: co-actors are mysteriously absent, as is any interplay between agent and context. As a consequence, the properties of the organizing system are overlooked, and reflection on access to resources, differentiated according to gender, as well as on gender-specific employment of rules, becomes difficult. Gendered facilities, norms (double standard) and interpretative schemes (gender stereotypes) are rendered invisible, as are the related organizing principles. Legitimation (assumed biological differences) and signification (socially constructed gender identities) together produce gender inequality. Although rules are different for women and men, female agents are held responsible for their own fate.

A restricted conception of agency, or the absence of a conceptualization of systems with their enabling and constraining structural properties, may have unintended consequences. The production and reproduction of gender, at the level of conduct, seems to be solely the business of individual women. Side by side victimization and blaming the victim seem to fit in the track of a 'personal characteristics' model.

Structural features

At the methodological level of institutions another model of analysis is found. Differences between women and men at school and university are explained in terms of 'structural factors'. Although structural factors have an inextricable interconnection with the social system, a meticulous examination makes differences become apparent. Some factors materialize incidentally, in special contexts, at specific moments in time/space. Others are part of a system's daily routine, and are continuously employed in social practices as rules and resources. By applying the theory of structuration, and especially the concept of system property to some 'structural factors' approaches, I will elucidate my statement.

Veeken (1982) finds three characteristics of the Dutch educational system, related to patterned gender differences at school and on the labor market, all detrimental to girls: the coexistence of two basic networks of education (general and vocational); the necessity to choose a limited combination of subjects at an early age; and, last but not least, coeducation. The coexistence of a vocational and a general network, and the necessity of choosing subjects can both be considered as embodiments of the system property of specialization. Coeducation is another system property, and will be dealt with later. Specialization as a system property is located in time/space. It will be employed in specific contexts – which I shall call *critical system moments* – when pupils are obliged to make decisions related to specialization. Here, the system property shows its dual character. To the individual pupil, opportunities are available to become an expert, and to gain access to certain sectors or segments of the labor market. Simultaneously, access to other segments is limited or even denied. The recursiveness of agency and structure, the located interplay between decision-making and specialization seem to be crucial here. The existence of two basic networks and the necessity to choose at critical system moments can be studied as two sides of the coin of specialization.

Koenders and Wolffensperger (1986) summarize structural constraints for female faculty: selection and assessment procedures and rewards turn out to be gender-biased. Moreover, within academia women are confronted with exclusion and outright neglect. Selection and assessment can be understood as embodiments of what is worth rewarding, and as manifestations of signification (as a structural principle), revealing its dual character at critical system moments within the university. At those moments, rewards are granted and denied, enabling a happy few to increase access to academic resources, and constraining the unlucky ones in their activities.

The second category of 'structural factors' is of a very different nature: they are continuously employed, as an integral part of practices, and do not show up incidentally, at certain important moments. Coeducation, for example, is a constituent element of the Dutch classroom. It materializes in teacher–pupil interaction, which is produced via able employment of rules and resources by both teachers and pupils. Research findings have demonstrated that, from kindergarten to the university lecture hall, female and male pupils are treated differently during lessons. When girls have good results, they are seen as having studied scrupulously. Bad results, on the other hand, are attributed to a lack of intellectual qualities. For boys, good results are credited to smartness or skill, bad results to laziness. Teachers foster gender-stereotyped assumptions about pupils and they act accordingly: girls are diligent but stupid, boys are clever but unwilling to work. Dweck et al. (1978) have demonstrated the impact on pupils' self-image and achievements of gendered interpretations and teacher behavior displayed during school hours. When treated in a manner usually reserved for girls, pupils of both sexes – girls *and* boys – begin to doubt their intellectual abilities. They all lose self-confidence. When teachers handle pupils in the way they usually treat boys, however, both sexes show a healthy increase in self-confidence. The double standard is harmful to girls and favorable to boys.

For at least 12 years, every Dutch pupil is part of a classroom situation six hours a day and five days a week. During those years, days and hours, girls and boys are educated together. In the classroom, teachers are in a power position. They have greater access to resources than pupils, which opens up the possibility to employ coeducation as a resource. If we conceptualize coeducation as a system property, teachers emerge who continuously use gender stereotypes as an interpretative scheme and double standards as a norm. In producing educational practices they produce gender differences to the detriment of girls.

Minority/majority ratios are also continuously employed as an integral part of practices. Within organizations they can be considered a system property, as a resource for those in a position of power. Members of a majority tend to interpret activities, abilities and achievements of a minority in terms of socially accepted stereotypes, and use double standards (Kanter 1977a,b). Ott (1985) has refined this theory: a lower status minority will suffer, whereas a higher status minority will benefit from stereotyping and double standards.[3] Within university, due to horizontal and vertical distributions of female and male faculty, in situated contexts like meetings, committee work etc. female faculty members are often outnumbered by males. Where 'female nature' is regarded as incompatible with real scientific work, female faculty members are perceived as women, and not as scientists or colleagues. Activities and accomplishments will be judged in terms of biology rather than seen as skills displayed and knowledge generated. 'She demonstrates an unhealthy detachment, an unfeminine rationality.' Or, on the contrary: 'She is too emotionally involved, which will damage scientific quality.' For members of a male majority, minority/majority ratios offer an opportunity to practice a double standard, thereby making female achievements – such as publications – invisible and irrelevant. For women, excellence and productivity are no guarantee of success. Female scientists have been cited less, and have been forgotten sooner, than male colleagues (Alic 1982; Kien and Cassidy 1984). The muting of female faculty decreases competition and enhances opportunities for remaining staff members. Science turns out to be male.

Coeducation and minority/majority ratios reflect gendered system properties of school and university respectively. For those with access to system resources, the possibility emerges to employ gendered rules in the course of daily conduct. In communication and sanctioning of everyday behavior, gender stereotypes are used and double standards practiced. Rules are different for women and men and, as a result, gender inequality is reproduced. When gendered rules are drawn on, women seem to suffer and men to benefit.

The notion of 'structural factors', used to explain gendered inequalities at the level of institutional analysis, generally lacks specificity. At school and university, system properties may vary in incidence and in consequence;

moreover, their relationship to gender can differ. 'Structural factors' have something in common though: they are setting boundaries to action. This reveals a second problem. Structure's constraining characteristics are illuminated at the expense of the knowledgeability and capability we have insisted on attributing to agency. Furthermore, the enabling side of structure, with a gender-differentiated access to resources and employment of gendered rules in its trail, becomes invisible.

At school and university, the dual character of structure and its relation to gender become evident. At critical system moments agents are obliged to choose; system properties bring about discursive decision-making, closing down or opening up avenues for future activities. Strategic conduct may prompt agents to avoid gender-stereotyped behavior and the twofold reproduction of patterned gender differences and social systems. The recursiveness of agency and structure functions differently in social practices. It is not so much discursive consciousness and decision-making that is important in this context, but rather practical knowledge of system properties, and the ability to draw on rules and resources in daily conduct. If gender, together with social system is employed, structural properties tend to differentiate between men and women. They turn out enabling for the first, and constraining for the last.

Dualism or duality

Voluntaristic and deterministic models, used to explain organized gender differences, both fail if it comes to conceptualizing power. One of the advantages of the theory of structuration is its three-dimensional approach to power *and* to communication and norms: 'Power intervenes conceptually between the broader notions of transformative capacity on the one side, and domination on the other' (Giddens 1979: 92). Power is defined in terms of agency, in terms of system properties (i.e. access to resources), and in terms of structural principles (i.e. domination). Transformative capacity is basic to agency and to the theory of structuration as a whole: 'Understood as transformative capacity, power is intrinsically related to human agency. The "could have done otherwise" of action is a necessary element of the theory of power' (Giddens 1979: 92).

Resources constitute the second pillar of Giddens' conceptualization of power. Access to resources in inter-action is a medium to effectuate capability on one hand, and to organize asymmetery on the other.

> Resources are the media whereby transformative capacity is employed as power in the routine course of social interaction; but they are at the same time structural elements of social systems as systems, reconstituted through their utilisation in social interaction. (Giddens 1979: 92)

Structural principles are described as follows: 'Structures of domination involve *asymmetries of resources employed* in the sustaining of power relations in and between systems of interaction' (Giddens 1979: 93; his emphasis).

In my critique of prevailing conceptual schemes, I have pointed out two major problems at the level of conduct. An adequate conceptualization of agency and a conception of contextuality are lacking. When a conception of agency is used in which capability is neglected, perceptions are distorted. How can girls, who – against nature and nurture – decide to specialize in physics and mathematics, in order to preserve options for a technical profession, be repre-sented at all by such a theory? How can female faculty staff who, because of career opportunities, decide to do research instead of teaching be perceived? If those who 'act otherwise' are rendered invisible, descriptions tend to emphasize passivity. A wanting conceptualization of agency, missing a notion of transformative capacity, is itself gendered in its consequences in the sense that it tends to produce a stereotyped 'femininity'. This may reinforce feelings of powerlessness in women. The theory of structuration escapes this risk by linking transformative capacity firmly to human agency.

According to Giddens, the 'study of context, or the contextuality of interaction, is inherent in the investigation of social reproduction' (Giddens 1984: 282). Structural properties are constituent elements of any context, being employed in interaction as rules and resources. Neglecting the contextuality of a phenomenon under study is harmful, even more so when gender is involved. When patterns of gender difference are explained in terms of biology or self-selection, rules and resources functioning as media of twofold reproduction stay hidden. Such an eclipse of organizing features tends to obscure asymmetries in access to resources and double standards in employment of rules. Under conditions of unequal access to resources, rules should be studied with special interest. Minority/majority ratios and coeducation represent a resource: male faculty staff, and teachers can hardly be prevented from setting gendered rules in communication and in administering sanctions. Where gender stereotypes are being drawn upon, gendered consequences are produced: feelings of insecurity in women and of self-assurance in men. A 'female identity' surfaces and, in the process, proves itself to be incompatible with brains. The opposite holds true for men.

Neglect of contextuality and unequal access to resources leads to questionable strategies for change. It might, for example, be wiser to 'de-program' teachers or faculty staff from gender stereotypes, than to influence decision-making of female pupils. If she plans to be an engineer, good marks for physics may not suffice, if double standards and asymmetrical access to resources according to gender are to be faced all the way to her profession. Individual strategic conduct does not guarantee success. A notion of contextuality, however, coupled with a conception of access to resources enhances balanced decision-making. It is a prerequisite to study the phenomenon of twofold reproduction: of the social system and of patterned gender differences, and to prevent the latter from taking place.

At the level of institutions, agency is overlooked completely. As a result, access to a resource, available to those involved in the development of strategies for change, is obscured. The practical and discursive knowledge of the person involved is invisible, as are the enabling characteristics of system properties. I have pointed out two types of structural properties of school and academia: critical system moments, and gendered rules and resources, continuously employed as an integral part of practices. Of both, constraining and enabling dimensions have been indicated. Critical system moments are conducive to a prolonged division of labor based on gender. They are at the same time, however, important for structural change. Because of the built-in obligation to make choices, these situated contexts are especially appropriate for increasing reflexivity, discursive consciousness and strategic conduct. Critical system moments enable actors to break gendered rules, and patterns of twofold reproduction. Especially at critical system moments they may choose to stop producing and reproducing patterns of gender differences tied to social systems.

Even if immunity to gender stereotyping and double standards is not guaranteed, and gender differences in access to resources are omnipresent, systematic and prolonged strategic conduct ultimately could lead to new organizing principles. The process to put an end to gender asymmetery will surely take its time. Meanwhile, a sound theoretical framework could be of help.

If we refuse to accept the mutual exclusiveness of agency and structure, and introduce recursiveness instead, social phenomena take on a new meaning. They turn into elements, constituting a more complex and complete picture of reality. Assumptions of knowledgeability and capability, and a conception of constraining *and* enabling sides of structure, can prevent dualism and its theoretical and political consequences. Awareness of transformative capacity, followed by a knowledgeable and capable employment of – existing and new – rules and resources, helps to transform the reproduction of male domination. A model in which transformative capacity, access to resources and domination are related to gender can aid the development of strategies for change. Under the condition that gender be built into its conceptual framework, the theory of structuration can be a useful theoretical model for women's studies, and a powerful resource for transformation.

Conclusion

Two questions have been raised in this chapter: how should an alliance between gender and social system be conceptualized, and is such an association to be expected in university education? The first question has been answered by introducing Giddens' conceptual scheme, supplemented by two new concepts: 'engendered structure' and 'twofold reproduction'. The concept of engendered structure served as a lever to grasp the interconnection of gender, agency and social system. Twofold reproduction refers to the simultaneous production and reproduction of social system and gender. For my discussion, I have chosen the two contexts of school and university. Common to both systems are patterned gender differences (horizontal and vertical distribution), and processes of twofold reproduction.

In the new concept of engendered structure, individual conduct and structural constraints have been related to gender, and to each other, thereby bridging the gap between voluntaristic and deterministic theoretical models. Gendered system properties are employed in interaction as unequal access to resources, double standards and gender stereotyping. They are used to produce social practices and at the same time differences between women and men. Gendered distributions are related to a gender-based division of labor, and to organizing principles involving domination, legitimation and signification.

In voluntaristic models, I have traced two major imperfections: capability and contextuality are lacking. In deterministic models, agency is overlooked all together, as is the enabling side of structure. To analyze the dynamics of agency, social system and gender in their full complexity, a model is needed which avoids the dangers of the Scylla of voluntarism and the Charybdis of determinism. The framework developed here may represent a first step. Transgressing the traditional subject–object dualism the way Giddens does, results in analyses of a more complex and complete nature. As a political advantage, this conceptual scheme prevents women from being blamed for their own situation or being portrayed as helpless victims.

In the process of structural change, individual transformative capacities must be translated into strategic conduct. Thus, an analysis of a system's gendered properties and its critical system moments, may become a resource. I have written this chapter in the hope that it may prove conducive to the development of this resource.

Notes

1 Taking the concept of knowledgeability seriously could have implications for feminist research (and education!). Scientific knowledge is surrounded by claims of truth and validity as is knowledge generated within women's studies. These claims are under severe feminist criticism (Smith 1979; Harding 1986). A consequence of the assumption of knowledgeability combined with feminist criticism could be a demand for different practices. Not only the knowledge of the women studied, but also that of the researcher herself should be part of the procedure.
2 From historical studies, assumptions of biological sex emerge as

arguments in public debates on equal educational rights for women. In the nineteenth and twentieth centuries, those debates show remarkable similarities. Both proponents and opponents of equal rights have based their arguments on the determining character of biology, and especially of female biology. 'Female nature' has been used to defend conflicting points of view on gender and education or on gender and science. Its aptness to be used to justify opposing positions is based on different interpretations of this biological mystery. During the first wave of the feminist movement in The Netherlands, 'female nature' was used as a weapon in the struggle for equal educational rights. Just as easily, however, it has been used in arguing against women's participation in higher and university education (Coutinho-Wiggelendam 1981). During the fifties, female biology appeared in the guise of 'female destiny', once again serving adversaries and advocates alike (Grotenhuis 1984). In debates on women and education, and on women and science, biological differences have legitimized opposing positions. Real or assumed biological differences have been deeply ingrained as a gender-organizing principle; they possibly still play their part in common sense and scientific knowledge.

3   Ott's findings demonstrate a different impact of gender-stereotyping and practicing of double standards for women and men. She has found that gender-stereotyping has negative results for women entering male domains of work (e.g. the police), but works out positively for men entering a female domain (e.g. the nursing profession).

PART THREE

SITES OF GENDERED POWER

5
Gender, Property and Power: *Mahr* and Marriage in a Palestinian Village
ANNELIES MOORS

The focus of this chapter is on the relations of power, property and gender. In theories of social stratification the concepts of property and power are intricately linked together. Two contending schools of thought have commented upon the way in which they are related. Political philosophers have seen property as grounded in power, while for political economists the order is reversed, with property as the central concept and power as derivative.[1] Comparatively little attention has been paid to the gender-specific aspects of the power–property nexus.

In anthropology, however, gender asymmetry was central in the work of the nineteenth-century thinkers whose interest focused on property rights, marriage forms and the position of women. Twentieth-century critics have largely dismissed their work because of their very limited access to field data and the strongly evolutionist perspective they employed.[2] Yet, the questions they raised about the relations among economy, kinship and gender have not been superseded. In contemporary British social anthropology similar topics are addressed, this time with recourse to extensive fieldwork material. Goody and Tambiah, for example, discuss at length how the transfer of property is linked both to social stratification and marriage systems. Like some of their nineteenth-century predecessors, their work stands within a materialist tradition, with property relations as their primary focus.

In this chapter I will first discuss the work of Goody and, to a lesser extent, Tambiah, focusing on those aspects which provide some insights into the relations among property, power and gender. This is followed by a presentation of empirical material derived from fieldwork in 1981 in Al-Balad, the fictive name of a village on the West Bank.[3] In the last part questions called forth by the case study are tied in with some more theoretical issues, in particular the way in which Goody conceptualizes gender asymmetry and the relations between power and property.

Goody and Tambiah on power, property and gender

Women in Al-Balad usually do not claim their inheritance share, but they may gain access to property through the gifts they receive when they marry. Marriage gifts and payments have traditionally been one of the central issues in anthropological theory. Anthropologists have, however, generally only paid attention to gifts exchanged for women. Marriage payments to women have largely been neglected.[4]

The work of Goody and Tambiah offers a broader perspective which explicitly focuses on the way in which marriage payments can be a medium for women to gain access to property. Their work seems also promising for a discussion on gender, property and power as they state that 'a concern with the interrelationship of the productive and reproductive systems, particularly as these affect the position of women' is central in their analysis (Goody and Tambiah 1973: preface). They link kinship and marriage with economy and politics, and aim at specifying these relations. Such a perspective avoids the public–private dichotomy, in which kinship and women are associated with the private, and economy and men with the public. In the case of Middle Eastern studies there is yet another advantage. In particular, Goody (1990) emphatically underlines the similarities between Asia and (pre-industrial) Europe. As such, his work can be seen as a powerful critique of the orientalist discourse which starts from a fundamental difference between the West and the Orient. Furthermore, his focus on productive systems is interesting in an area which has been dominated by a strongly culturalist perspective.

In *Bridewealth and Dowry* (1973) Goody and Tambiah set out to emphasize the fundamental differences between these two systems of marriage payments and the consequences this has for women's access to property. Although superficially they might appear as each other's mirror image, bridewealth being paid by the kin of the groom and dowry by the bride's side, they are of a different order. Bridewealth is a transaction in which wealth passes horizontally, from the male kin of the groom to the male kin of the bride. It is part of a circulating pool of resources, as a man can, for example, marry using the bridewealth paid for his sister. Dowry, on the other hand, passes vertically, usually from father to daughter, and becomes part of the conjugal fund of the new couple. Dowry goes with the bride, and can be seen as a form of female property, a kind of pre-mortem inheritance. The *mahr*, as the marriage payments in the Islamic world are called, has often been categorized as bridewealth because the bridal gifts are paid for by the groom's side. Goody and Tambiah (1973), however, classify the *mahr* as a type of dowry, because it is not part of a circulating fund, but functions as starting capital for the new couple. Goody calls it an 'indirect dowry' as the bride receives the gifts from the groom, and not from her father.

Goody and Tambiah place marriage payments within the wider context of the transfer of property and relate the payment of bridewealth and dowry to different productive systems. On the basis of differences in agricultural technology and land scarcity, Goody and Tambiah (1973) create a dichotomy, with Africa south of the Sahara on the one hand, and Europe and Asia, taken together, on the other. Sub-Saharan Africa is characterized by little economic differentiation, as technology is simple and land plentiful. Inheritance there is homogeneous (it stays within the lineage), with property generally transferred only through the male line and bridewealth is paid, forming a circulating fund. Bridewealth is regarded as a compensation for the loss of the labor and childbearing capacities of a woman. In 'Eurasia', on the other hand, intensification of agriculture brings greater economic differentiation. In these hierarchical societies parents are concerned with maintaining the status of their male *and* female children. Property is (bilaterally) transferred to both sons and daughters, daughters often receiving (part of) their inheritance share as a dowry. Through settlement of property they aim at an equal match (often through in-marriage) and to uphold the prestige of the family.

In *Production and Reproduction* Goody (1976) further works out the relation between women's access to property, women's work in agriculture and their position in society. He concurs with Boserup (1970), who argues that in extensive hoe agriculture women are more involved in agricultural labor than men, while in extensive plow agriculture it is mainly the men who work in agriculture. Women in sub-Saharan Africa are food producers, they have a certain economic autonomy and freedom of movement. This is in contrast to the 'Eurasian' male agricultural system, where women are basically seen as the mothers of heirs to property. In that case marriages need to be carefully balanced, women's sexuality is strictly controlled, women are economically dependent and men are obliged to provide.

In their later work the dichotomy between African women with some economic autonomy and the secluded and dependent 'Eurasian' women is modified to some extent. Goody (1990) points to social differences within hierarchical societies. As among the lower groups large transfers of property are not the main focus of marriage, joint families are less common, there is more conjugality, control of the choice of marriage partner is less strict, women are less secluded and women's work is more important than among the higher groups. Tambiah (1989) elaborates on the complex nature of women's position.[5] African women have more economic autonomy than higher strata Indian women and their sexuality is less strictly controlled, yet, in his view, it does not necessarily follow that patriarchal domination is stronger in India than in Africa. While African women as producers of food have indeed some economic independence, they can only expect limited financial support from their husbands and usually do not control land. This places them in a vulnerable position. Indian high-caste women on the other hand, are secluded and economically dependent, yet, as their husbands are obliged to provide for them and their children, they are also protected, and they can have some access to property through the dowry.

Goody and Tambiah's work gives us some insights about women's access to property through dowry or inheritance in relation to social stratification, women's labor in agriculture and the implications this has for asymmetries between men and women. Yet, the way in which Goody and Tambiah analyze 'women's position' in different societies is problematic and to some extent contradictory. Before elaborating on these issues, I will first turn to the empirical material and describe women's access to property in Al-Balad.

Al-Balad: from subsistence agriculture to male labor migration

The village of Al-Balad is situated in the eastern part of the Jabal Nablus, a mountainous area with fertile plains, where dry-farming agriculture is dependent on irregular rainfall.[6] Until the mid 1950s most villagers made a living from agriculture, which was largely directed towards subsistence. The majority of the households in Al-Balad were semi-independent smallholders. In addition, livestock was an important source of livelihood with households spending part of winter and spring with their flocks in the mountains. From the early 1930s onward, a small number of men from Al-Balad set out to migrate temporarily to the coastal areas in search of employment. But income from migratory labor only supplemented that from agriculture.

With the creation of the state of Israel in 1948 migration to the coastal areas was cut off. From the early 1950s onwards, migration eastward started and a rapidly growing number of men from Al-Balad went to work in the Gulf States (Kuwait in particular) and in Jordan (the East Bank). The Israeli occupation of the West Bank in 1967 further induced migration abroad, and wage labor in Israel became a new source of employment. Access to land diminished when in 1970 a large fertile plain belonging to Al-Balad, where wheat and barley were cultivated, was confiscated. The size and number of the flocks also dwindled because the mountainous lands, where animals used to be tended, were declared a closed military area. Yet, most village households still have access to some land where they mainly grow wheat, barley and olives for household consumption. In contrast to the 1930s, however, dry-farming with its seasonal labor demands has now become an adjunct to wage labor instead of vice versa and most households are largely dependent on male wage labor in Israel, Jordan or the Gulf States.

These transformations in the economic structure of the village have influenced the gender division of labor. When agriculture was still the main source of livelihood both men and women were involved in agricultural labor. There was a certain gender division of labor, but only the women from the influential families did not work on the land. Large-scale male migration has not resulted in women taking over male tasks. With individual households having less access to land and livestock than previous generations the demand for agricultural labor has decreased.[7] As limiting women's work in agriculture is deemed prestigious, other men in the household are preferred to take over the tasks of the migrant. Also, many migrants return to the village regularly and remain involved in agriculture or, in particular if they work in the Gulf States, their income allows them to mechanize and employ male wage labor for specific short-term tasks on their holdings.[8]

Yet, even though women have not taken over male tasks, there has been an important shift in the relative labor input of men and women in agriculture. In comparison with men the workload of women has increased, since it is primarily men's work, such as plowing and threshing grain, which has been mechanized, while women still weed and harvest by hand, plant vegetables and process milk (into cheese). This transformation of subsistence agriculture (of both men and women) to migration wage labor, while women remain involved in agriculture, has had important consequences for the access of women to property.

The *mahr* and women's access to productive property

When agriculture was still the main source of livelihood and the market for land and labor was limited, kinship and marriage were central to the reproduction of property relations. Residence was patri(viri)local, with households largely constituted along lines of patrilineal descent.[9] When a woman married, she left her natal household, moving in with her in-laws. Most of the household property was controlled by the eldest male and a son was financially dependent upon his father. A father, on the other hand, was expected to provide housing, food and clothing for all members of the household. He was also responsible for paying the *mahr* for brides for his sons.

In the rural areas of Palestine, women generally only claimed their inheritance rights in specific cases, in particular, if they did not have brothers. They considered it shameful to 'take land from their brothers', as a man ought to provide for the family and a woman is supposed to be provided for. By not claiming their inheritance share they held a life-long claim of rights of sustenance from their father's house. Yet, although they owned considerably less land and livestock than men, women in Al-Balad were not totally excluded from access to productive property. This they acquired mainly through marriage gifts, the *mahr*.

While in Islamic law the whole *mahr* belongs to the bride,[10] in the 1930s and 1940s a bride in Al-Balad would usually receive about one-third of it and her father would keep the remainder himself, sometimes using it to get a son married. It was this bridal share which could be a potential source of productive property for women. As a standard procedure part of it was used to buy household goods, but most of it was spent on gold, particularly gold coins. Women had considerable control over their gold. Acquiring gold was often the beginning of a whole series of transactions. Women bought and sold gold, cows, goats and, to a lesser extent, land, depending on the market. In other cases women had direct access to productive property. Although as a rule the *mahr* was paid in cash, before the late 1950s this was not always easy. Few men in Al-Balad were engaged in wage labor, so the amount had to be saved from the sale of agricultural surplus and livestock. Thus, it could happen that the father of the groom offered a piece of land, a number of olive trees or some goats as *mahr*. Especially for a young bride it could be difficult to have *de facto* control over land, as she often moved in with her in-laws, the 'previous owners' of the land. But after they died, especially if she were widowed, she could gain considerable control.

Yet, marriage did not imply access to property for all women. Until the late 1950s exchange marriages (*badal*) occurred regularly in Al-Balad.[11] In that case the son and daughter of one family married the daughter and son of another, or occasionally a widower exchanged his daughter for a new wife. Either no *mahr* was paid or the bride received a share which was considerably less than the usual.[12]

When in the 1950s (migration) wage labor became increasingly important as a source of livelihood this resulted in less control of fathers over sons and influenced the way in which property was transferred between generations. No longer is the extended family seen as the ideal. Young men, often strongly supported by their wives, strive to move into a new house as soon as possible after marriage and are able to set up their own households earlier than before. This greater autonomy of sons expresses itself in the earlier transfer of (part of) the property from father to son. A father often helps his son substantially by giving him a piece of land to build on and by financially supporting the construction of the house.

With changes in men's relation to property, the access of women to property has also been transformed. The father's share of the *mahr* has gradually disappeared, and the bride has received an increasing part of the *mahr* herself. From the 1950s on, brides generally received one-half, then two-thirds and since the early 1970s most brides receive the whole *mahr* themselves. Their fathers do not take anything from it and in a few cases even add to it. In addition, more women have access to property through the *mahr*, as with the increase in cash income exchange marriages without or with a very low *mahr* have virtually disappeared.[13]

At the same time, however, the relative value of the *mahr* has declined. Male wages have increased much faster, thus men do not have to work as long as before in order to pay the *mahr*.[14] Furthermore, the nature of the *mahr* has also changed, with the result that women's access to property, in particular to productive property, has actually decreased. Since cash is more readily available, women no longer receive livestock or land directly as part of the bride's share. Most importantly, however, since the middle of the 1960s fewer and fewer women sell their *mahr* gold to buy land and livestock. One reason is that since land prices have risen much faster than the bride's share, women have less opportunity to buy this type of property. The main point is, however, that with male migration the difference in the nature of the work men and women perform has been emphasized. Only men are directly incorporated in the market economy and have access to cash, while buying goods for consumption in the market has become much more important than previously. In this way, a hierarchical division between wage labor and subsistence labor has developed, with unpaid labor valued less, and, to a larger extent, allocated to women. The result of these transformations is that women are seen more as consumers than as producers. This greater emphasis on men as providers and women as (unproductive) consumers in itself discourages independent property ownership by women. If a woman sells her gold now, she usually does so to help her husband build a house, to set him up in a small business, or to help him with the initial costs of migration.

In line with these developments another change in *mahr* payments has taken place. In the early 1980s for the first time a token *mahr* of 1 JD (Jordanian Dinar) was registered in the marriage contracts in Al-Balad. This quickly gained in popularity. In the case of a token *mahr* the costs for the groom are not lower, as he must still give the bride the gifts which she otherwise would have bought with her *mahr*. Yet, he has more control over the nature of the gifts.

In short, while young men have become less dependent on their fathers, women's dependency on men has increased. With a large part of the household income derived from male wage labor and women working in subsistence agriculture, women have increasingly become defined as unproductive consumers. This has resulted both in a relative decline in female access to property and in less female control over property.

Transformations in the organization of marriage

Since the *mahr* is women's main route to property owner-ship, the other side of property is marriage. When production was still primarily directed towards subsistence, kinship and marriage were central both for the transfer of property and the allocation of labor. But marriage had a different meaning for men than for women.[15] A man needed a wife to do 'women's work', but especially to give him sons who would help and support him in his old age. For women, marriage was somewhat less necessary. If a woman did not marry, a male relative was obliged to provide for her. In emotional terms delaying marriage could be advantageous, as an unmarried woman continued living with her own relatives, of whom more support and sympathy were to be expected than of her in-laws. Yet, the long-term prospects for an older, unmarried woman were not very positive. If she did marry, it often was a less prestigious marriage, with an elderly widower or perhaps as the second wife in a polygynous household. If she still was unmarried when her parents died, she would have to live with her brother's wife, and the contrasts between herself as an unmarried women and her sister-in-law as 'the mother of sons' would become increasingly visible.

Depending on gender and kinship position, individuals could have divergent marriage preferences. With unmarried women seen as a threat to the social order, there was strong pressure on women to marry and to marry young. While accepting marriage, girls disliked being married at a very young age or to a much older man.[16] Concerning marriage age, there might well be a conflict of interest between a girl (often supported by her mother) and her future mother-in-law. It could be the groom's mother who wanted her son to marry young in order to bring female labor into the household or because it would be easier for her to influence a very young bride.

Culturally, patrilineal endogamy was highly valued. Ideally, bride and groom were related through males. A man could put a claim on his father's brother's daugther (his *bint 'amm*) and the *mahr* to be paid for such a marriage was often lower.[17] Girls themselves generally preferred marrying within the village and within the lineage, expecting less affection from strangers. But they also had their specific marriage preferences, which could contradict lineage and village endogamy. Young women may prefer a partner related through females. If a girl married her *ibn khala* (mosiso), her mother-in-law would be the sister of her mother with whom she was expected to have good relations. If she married her *ibn 'amm* (fabrso), her mother-in-law and her own mother were *salafat* (women married to brothers), a relation culturally defined as potentially strained. Also, a mother might like to marry her sons and daughters to her own relatives in order to reconfirm her relationship with them.

In the organization of marriages mothers had some influence based on the social segregation between men and women, but it was the father who in the end decided when and whom a son or daughter would marry. An important consequence of the new social division of labor is that fathers have less material control over the organization of marriages. Nevertheless, a young man is still dependent on his family to arrange his marriage. With fathers less in control, mothers are more able to influence marriage arrangements. The interests of mothers and mothers-in-law may still be contradictory, but as households now tend to split up in an earlier phase of the household cycle the institution of the 'mother-in-law' has become less central. As a result more girls succeed in delaying marriage, the social preference for kinship through men is less accentuated and refusing a suitor, also if he is an *ibn 'amm*, has become easier.[18] While women in Al-Balad have less control over property and have become economically more dependent on men, they have gained some autonomy in marriage organization.

Some comments on Goody's work

As stated previously, the work of Goody and Tambiah is important because they recognize the capacity of women to hold property and focus on the connections between kinship and economy. Yet the way in which they analyze the relation between gender asymmetry and property is problematic. This can be illuminated by contrasting the description of historical transformations of women's access to property and marriage organization in Al-Balad with the relations Goody specifies about property and marriage.

Turning to the empirical material, the Al-Balad data show some flaws in Goody's conceptualization of the *mahr*. He classifies the *mahr* as an 'indirect dowry' as property is transferred vertically to form a conjugal fund: 'the ultimate recipient of these gifts is the bride and not her kin . . . the bulk goes to the bride herself and thus forms part of a joint (or sometimes separate) conjugal fund' (Goody 1973: 2). In his later work Goody (1990) acknowledges that marriage transactions in Arab societies are not necessarily identical. Yet, he rejects the possible occurrence of marriage payments with some similarity to bridewealth in this area.[19]

Islamic law indeed stipulates that a *mahr* ought to be paid to the bride or to her representative on her behalf. But in Al-Balad practice has been very different. The *mahr* was not always paid and the bride was not always the main beneficiary as a bride's father only gave part of the *mahr* to his daughter. In other words, the *mahr* seems to be a rather flexible institution which depending on its local and historical context can have both bridewealth and dowry aspects.

If we recognize that the *mahr* is historically specific, there are some interesting paradoxes concerning Goody's theory and the transformations that have taken place in Al-Balad. We might define this shift as one from marriage payments with bridewealth aspects, to something more akin to an indirect dowry. While the earlier *mahr* with its large father's share did partly function as a (limited) circulating fund, at present property is transferred vertically. Increasingly, the bride's father gives the whole *mahr* to his daughter, and in a few cases even adds to it. In Goody's perspective it is the dowry which gives women access to property. In Al-Balad, however, a greater emphasis on the dowry side of the *mahr* has coincided with a relative decrease of women's access to and control over property. We encounter a similar contrast when considering women's work in agriculture. While Goody follows Boserup in linking bridewealth to female farming systems and dowry to male farming, in Al-Balad we see a shift toward indirect dowry coinciding with a relatively higher female labor input in agriculture. Thirdly, Goody links strict parental control over marriages to dowry systems. In Al-Balad, however, with the *mahr* increasingly becoming an indirect dowry women have gained some space in the arrangement of marriages.

The main point is that the meaning of marriage and the *mahr* in Al-Balad in the early 1980s was very different from that in the 1930s. Yet, Goody constructs dichotomies, such as those of bridewealth and dowry, without paying attention to the various meanings similar institutions can have in different contexts. This ties in with the nature of his materialist approach. In Goody's view it is agricultural technology and land scarcity which determine whether the division of (landed) property is egalitarian or hierarchical and whether bridewealth or dowry is paid. It is this dichotomy which ultimately determines 'the position of women'.

Such a perspective is problematic as the exclusive focus on the property side of productive systems tends to neglect the importance of labor. Yet, the shifts in the meaning of marriage and the *mahr* in Al-Balad are intrinsically linked to changes in the social and gender division of labor. When production was mainly directed toward subsistence, marriages were not only important for the transfer of property but also for the allocation of labor. With male migration this is less so, and it is within this context that women have gained some autonomy in marriage organization. At the same time women's relative labor input has increased, but women's labor is less valued. Women have become defined as consumers and this has resulted in less female access to property.

Furthermore, Goody's conceptualization of property is partial. In his theory he treats property as a material resource, with power deriving from property relations. But, as Whitehead (1984) has emphasized, property is in itself a social relation. It refers not only to material resources, but also to relations between people. This means that it is not sufficient to elaborate on the consequences of property ownership for power relations between men and women. We also ought to examine the differences in the way society constructs men's and women's capacity to act in regard to property. When production in Al-Balad was directed toward subsistence, women had access to property, yet the relation of men and women to (productive) property was defined differently. Men were already defined as providers, which entitled them to put a claim on female labor. This labor did not give women any specific rights to the produce, as consumption was organized according to hierarchies of age and gender. Women who owned property did not have similar claims to male labor. Furthermore, women's access to property was mediated through the marriage system. The very same *mahr* that gave women access to property reinforced the dominance of fathers in the marriage system.

In fact, when gender is involved, Goody himself deviates from his model in which power is derived from property. Implicitly he takes male dominance as a point of departure. In his discussions on egalitarian and hierarchical systems, a society is 'egalitarian' if property is divided equally among *men*. In hierarchical societies a dowry is paid through which women have access to property and such societies often have male farming systems with women economically dependent on men. These statements can only be reconciled if male domination is presupposed. The same problem comes up when we turn to Goody's discussion on who receives the dowry. On the one hand, a dowry (in contrast to bridewealth) means female property ownership. On the other hand, Goody sees the household as a property-holding unit, with the dowry functioning as a conjugal fund under the control of the husband.[20]

In short, Goody's work points to the importance of linking kinship and economy, but does not help us in specifying the relations among gender, power and property. This is due to the nature of his materialist approach, with production reduced to property, and property reduced to a material resource. Insufficient attention is paid to labor and the way in which property is structured by or is a result of relations of power. Furthermore, when in the case of gender relations the power–property relation is reversed, male dominance is taken for granted. For feminist studies, a perspective in which neither the meaning of the *mahr* nor gender asymmetry is taken as a given, seems more promising. The point would then be to question how in a specific context marriage payments are related to women's access to property relations and gender asymmetry.

Notes

This research has been supported by the Foundation for Social and Cultural Sciences, which is subsidized by The Netherlands Organization for Scientific Research (NWO).

1   For an elaborate discussion of the relation of property to power see Pels (1986).

2   Yet one of the bestknown works, Engels (1884), has had a strong impact on feminist studies. See, for example, Hirshon (1984), the first collection of essays focusing explicitly on gender and property. For a critical review of his work see Sayers et al. (1987).

3   This material has previously been presented in Moors (1990).

4   This is the case in different anthropological traditions, where 'women as actors' are largely neglected. Radcliffe-Brown only pays attention to the rights men gain over women (see Caplan 1984), Meillassoux defines women as 'the means of reproduction' (see Harris and Young 1981) and for Lévi-Strauss the exchange of women is a structural principle (see MacCormack 1980).

5   Tambiah (1989) modifies the theses of *Bridewealth and Dowry* to some extent. He limits the discussion of dowry to the higher social strata in Northern India as amongst the non-propertied strata of 'Eurasia' dowry is less common. He admits that dowry cannot be seen as pre-mortem inheritance, because the content seems to depend more upon the status of the groom, than on the property of the household of origin. He also qualifies the idea that dowry forms part of the conjugal fund of the marrying couple, as part of it is appropriated by the joint family. Yet, in his view, the original theses of *Bridewealth and Dowry* remain unshaken. In propertied India, property is transferred 'to and through both males and females and this transmission emphasizes vertical bonds between parents and children at the cost of lateral lineage bonds' (Tambiah 1989: 426).

6   Some of the inhabitants of Al-Balad also had access to irrigated land in the Wadi Far'a, less than ten kilometers away from the village. The discussion here is, however, limited to the majority of households in the village with access to dry-farming land only.

7   Households also gradually lost access to land due to the system of partible inheritance.

8   It needs to be underlined that such was the situation in 1981. In the following years, the economic recession, also in the Gulf States, has meant less income from abroad, and increased political repression has made it more difficult for migrants to return to the occupied territories. Also, with the *intifada*, new emphasis has been placed on self-reliance and working the land. Again the Gulf War has greatly affected the situation of Palestinian (migrant) labor. To what extent these developments may have influenced the gender division of labor in agriculture and women's access to property is not discussed here.

9   The Arabic term for household in this region, *dar*, is also used for 'house' and for 'lineage'.

10 In Islamic law, the term *mahr* refers to the amount registered in the marriage contract which the groom has to pay to the bride or her

marriage contract which the groom has to pay to the bride or her representative. At present, the *mahr* in this region is subdivided into the prompt dower (to be paid at marriage), the deferred dower (to be paid in case of death of husband or divorce) and the *tawabi'* (description of furniture the husband provides). In this paper the term *mahr* refers to the prompt dower only.

11 In a sample of 35 marriages in the period 1928–1961, approximately one-quarter to one-third of all marriages were *badal*.

12 These marriages often were an indication of poverty. Also, when a regular *mahr* had been paid, the result of poverty could be that a woman had to sell her gold in order to be able to feed her children.

13 In a sample of 40 marriages in the period 1961–1981, about 10 per cent of all marriages were *badal*. Furthermore, in these cases of *badal* a regular *mahr* was usually paid.

14 In addition, a comparison of the transfers at or shortly after marriage from a father to his son, with those to his daughter-in-law (the *mahr*), shows the lesser importance of the *mahr*.

15 The following description of marriage organization in Al-Balad is similar to Granqvist's work (1931, 1935). Granqvist did fieldwork in 1927 in Artas, a village near Bethlehem.

16 They strongly disapproved of marriage to a much older man, as such a man was presumed to be very dominant and affection was more likely to develop between husband and wife if the age differential was small.

17 In such marriages, property would stay in the lineage, even in cases in which a woman would inherit.

18 In a sample of 20 marriages in the period 1928–1948, about half of the brides were married when younger than 16 years; almost a third were younger than 14. In a sample of 30 marriages in the period 1967–1981, no woman was married younger than 14 years; three were younger than 16.

19 On the basis of very limited evidence, mainly from North Africa and North Yemen, Goody dismisses the work of authors who 'dealing with Palestine have asserted that the gifts from the groom's family are said to be used by the bride's family to acquire their own brides' by simply stating that 'in most parts of the Near East that is not the case' (Goody 1990: 375).

20 Such an indifference to the gender of the recipient is remarkable as for Goody the main point of dowry systems is that property is transferred to both men and women. Even if the bride receives the *mahr* herself, it is questionable whether an indirect dowry implies divergent devolution. Since the bride receives the *mahr* from her husband and/or his father, with her sons inheriting from her, at most the *mahr* is a temporary diversion from patrilineal transmission. If, however, it is her husband who is really in control, even that is not the case.

6
Sovereign and Disciplinary Power: a Foucaultian Analysis of the Chilean Women's Movement
RIET DELSING

To Julieta Kirkwood

My interest in the Chilean women's movement stems from a personal involvement during the post-Allende years. The first period after the military coup of 1973 in Chile was marked by a climate of fear and bewilderment, as we witnessed the systematic destruction of Chilean political, social, cultural and economic life. Our days were spent trying to counteract these effects through church organizations, clandestine political parties and trade unions.

It was in this context that the first women's groups emerged: women looking for their missing husbands, sons and fathers; women defending their imprisoned or exiled family members; women getting together in workshops and soup kitchens in order to meet their basic needs in a rapidly worsening economic situation; and, in later years, women protesting in the streets against the dictator, demanding 'bread, work, justice and freedom'.

In the process of uniting around these specific issues, we were becoming aware that our malaise was not only due to the dictatorship. Through the mere act of organizing, we found ourselves clashing both with the representatives of the regime and with our supposed allies, our *compañeros* in the struggle for the restoration of democracy and socialism. It was this clash which initiated a process of reflection among a growing number of women on why they were continually finding themselves taking secondary roles in the political decision-making process.

In order to reach greater understanding of this pheno-menon, it seems important to make a historical analysis of women's participation in the public sphere. Doing this we find that, during the first half of this century, there existed a constant friction between organized women on one hand and the state and political parties on the other. While women felt that their specific interests were not being represented by official politics, they also had an ambivalent attitude as to what shape their political participation should take.

In this chapter I propose that Foucault's reflections on power and power relations can provide interesting insights into the reasons for women's scarce participation in government bodies and political parties in Chile in the past and present.[1] Special attention is given to his analysis of the interrelatedness of sovereign and disciplinary power, to his critique of orthodox Marxism and to his ideas about new forms of power.

Foucault on power

Foucault became interested in the phenomenon of power and power relations after the student revolt of May 1968 in Paris, where new modes of political struggle were deve-loped, creating new lines of political and philosophical thought among the French left. Foucault maintains that before 1968 the concrete mechanisms of power had never been analyzed: 'This task could only begin after 1968, that is to say, on the basis of daily struggles at grass roots level' (Foucault 1980: 116).[2] Three aspects of his theory are relevant for the arguments I want to develop in this chapter, beginning with his theory of sovereignty and disciplinary discourses.[3]

According to Foucault, 'right' in the West has traditionally been the king's right. Royal power was invested in laws made by jurists. This body of laws developed into a discourse, in which the appearance was created that laws were the embodiment of 'truth'. Foucault points out the latent brutality of the domination inherent in royal power and shows 'right' to be the instrument of this domination. The essential function of the discourse of 'right' has been to efface the domination intrinsic to royal power in order to legitimate rights of sovereignty and create a legal obligation to obey. The theory of sovereignty that requires obedience can also be seen as a practice of domination based on techniques of subjugation. This theory was the leading principle of state power in the West from the time of feudal societies until the advent of parliamentary democracies, when it became the organizing principle for the new legal codes of the nineteenth century.

In the seventeenth and eighteenth centuries, a different kind of power emerged:

This new mechanism of power is more dependent upon bodies and what they do, than upon the Earth and its products. It is a mechanism of power which permits time and labour, rather than wealth and commodities to be extracted from bodies. (Foucault 1980: 104)

This kind of power is based on discipline rather than sovereignty and calls for survelliance. A series of disciplinary discourses began to develop in mental hospitals, clinics, barracks, factories, schools and families, aimed at shaping people's minds and bodies.

Modern society is characterized by a juridical discourse based on public right as well as a number of simultaneously occurring disciplinary discourses. 'Sovereignty and disciplinary mechanisms are two absolutely integral constituents of the general mechanism of power in our society' (Foucault 1980: 108). Although disciplinary discourses may speak of a rule, it is not in the juridical sense as derived from sovereignty, but in the sense of a natural rule, a 'norm'.

The next aspect of Foucault's theory I am concerned with is his critique of orthodox Marxist conceptions about the role of the state and the Marxist failure to link state power to disciplinary discourses. Orthodox Marxist parties have been concerned with the overthrow of existing political power structures. Orthodox Marxist theory foresees the reversal of power relations of the ruling and the proletarian classes with their ultimate elimination in communism. This reversal will take place through class struggle and a takeover of the state apparatus, resulting first in the dictatorship of the proletariat and, subsequently, the disintegration of the state.

Taking up an argument put forth by early opponents of Marx, Foucault maintains that the ultimate elimination of power relations (the classless society) will never come about if the mechanisms of domination are merely repeated. Seizing the state apparatus is self-defeating, since it means the appropriation of the very system we want to abolish. If our goal is the ultimate elimination of power relations, the state apparatus is part of the problem. Foucault sees an example of the failures of this strategy in the contemporary pre-Gorbachev Soviet state, which suffered from an 'empirical non-correspondence between the level of discourses and the level of historical effects' (Gordon in Foucault 1980: 248). The postulates of the Marxist discourse were not being put into practice in the Soviet state, where power relations were maintained and intensified in state bureaucracy and supported by techniques of domination, inherent in the system.

Foucault also criticizes orthodox Marxism for not making the connection between the principle of sovereignty as the locus of power in the modern state and other, parallel systems of domination based on disiplinary mechanisms. Thus, Foucault identifies two shortcomings in orthodox Marxist theory. It is not only deficient in providing a way to achieve its own purpose, a classless society; it also fails to recognize the importance of the analysis of disciplinary discourses. This becomes particularly problematic because of the hegemonic orthodox interpretations of Marxist theory which have come to play a role in progressive and radical analyses of Chilean society.

A third set of ideas, developed by Foucault, is the creation of alternative power mechanisms, which can break through both state power based on the theory of sovereignty, and parallel disciplinary power mechanisms based on disciplinary discourses. First, he proposes a new theory in which discursive knowledge is opposed to strategic knowledge:

> The role for theory today seems to me to be just this: not to formulate the global systematic theory which holds everything in place, but to analyse the specificity of mechanisms of power, to locate the connections and extensions, to build little by little a strategic knowledge [*savoir*]. (Foucault 1980: 145)

This new kind of theoretical production should be autonomous, non-centralized and not dependent on the approval of the established regimes of thought (Foucault 1980: 81). The role of the intellectual in this is no longer central, but rather that of an adviser: 'The project, tactics and goals to be adopted are a matter for those who do the fighting' (Foucault 1980: 62). Foucault's proposal for a course of action is twofold:

1 To investigate, historically and in the present, beginning from the lowest levels, how concrete mechanisms of power function, in the materiality of ongoing subjugation.
2 To build strategies for change during and on the basis of such an analysis; that is, to learn and to learn to act upon what we see (the effects), and not on what we think we should see (the discourse).

Foucault also argues that the sovereignty of the state, legal codes and the disciplinary mechanisms that sustain them should be replaced by a completely different *power principle*. He hints at this kind of power when he says that 'power is neither given, nor exchanged, but rather exercised, and ... only exists in action' (Foucault 1980: 89), and '[power] needs to be considered as a productive network which runs through the whole social body, much more than as a negative instance whose function is repression' (Foucault 1980: 119). Foucault thus proposes that we should study the concrete power mechanisms that sustain state power and, simultaneously, build strategies for change aimed at establishing *power networks* which are essentially antidisciplinarian and non-coercive.

Feminism, Foucault and power

The three aspects of Foucault's theory outlined above – disciplinary mechanisms of power versus state power, Marxism's focus on state power and the creation of alternative power mechanisms – can be linked to feminist theory. The resulting insights may shed light on aspects of the history of the Chilean women's movement.

First of all, Foucault does not pay much attention to gender in his reflections on power. One of his few references to relations between the sexes is:

The Family, even now, is not a simple reflection or extension of the power of the State; it does not act as the representative of the State in relation to children, just as the male does not act as its representative with respect to the female. For the State to function in the way it does, there must be, between male and female or adult and child, quite specific relations of domination, which have their own configuration and relative autonomy. (Foucault 1980: 187)

In this passage, Foucault clearly hints at the power relations between man and woman as reinforcing state power. These power relations can be seen as the basic ingredient of the system of gender subordination based on the discourse of gender. It is my contention that gender ideology is a disciplinary discourse running parallel to and reinforcing state power. As we saw, disciplinary discourses are based on norms or natural rules. Gender ideology is saturated with such natural rules for women, in their roles of mothers, sexual partners and housekeepers. An important feature of the gender discourse (as well as of other disciplinary discourses) is its assimilation by the actors involved. Both women and men internalize the gender discourse. Feminists are slowly but surely uncovering this mechanism and directing their theory and practice toward its dissolution.

Like Foucault, feminists have criticized the orthodox Marxists' stance that the 'real' struggle is the class struggle and the takeover of the state apparatus. Orthodox Marxists argue that the 'woman question' will be resolved in that process or, at the very latest, after the revolution has taken place.[4] Such thinking has generally, but particularly in Latin America, slowed the politicization process of women and obstructed the recognition of gender subordination as a separate system of domination. As Juliet Mitchell notes:

> It has traditionally been held on the left that women can get 'equal rights', in a bourgeois revolution, under capitalism, and . . . political demands that women make can be accommodated in the prevailing system, and hence are 'reformist' . . . This position is a mirror reflection of how women's issues are being seen within the bourgeois society itself, i.e. as not the real issue. (Mitchell 1971: 72)

Foucault takes issue with the practice of posing a hierarchy of 'real issues', when he states that 'nothing in society will be changed if the mechanisms of power that function outside, below and alongside the state apparatuses, on a much more minute and everyday level, are not also changed' (Foucault 1980: 60). A second point is that Marxist men have not been sufficiently aware that they are simultaneously part of the class and gender systems, which makes them subject to, while at the same time exercising, power. This has seriously hampered women in the construction of their movement. Not only are they victims of hidden violence at home, exercised by their Marxist comrades; there are also numerous examples of violence against women in the public sphere, for example, within the New Left when the movement was just beginning (Mitchell 1971: 85, 86).

It is Foucault's contention that it is not fruitful to look at the world through the focus of grand theories and that we should attempt to acquire 'strategic knowledge' instead. This is echoed in feminist notions concerning the desirability of relating theory and practice: 'Theory follows from practice and is impossible to develop in the absence of practice' (Chester 1979: 60).[5] Since the 1960s feminists have put forward the notion that: ' "the personal is political". Within that phrase is condensed the understanding that the seemingly most intimate details of private existence are actually structured by larger relations' (Ross and Rapp 1981: 51). In this way, the notion of what 'politics' means is broadened, offering the possibility of political action on matters formerly considered to be 'private' and, thus, outside the realm of politics. In the private sphere, feminists have been trying to combat the concrete, everyday power mechanisms of gender subordination – the same kinds of mechanisms Foucault has identified in other fields.

In the second wave of the feminist movement, there has been strong emphasis on horizontal, loose-knit organizations aimed at giving all participants an equal part in the analysis of their situations. After initial concerns with consciousness-raising groups (see Mitchell 1971), a renewed interest can be discerned in recent years for 'networking' (a strictly horizontal way of organizing) as one of the most important political and strategic tools of a growing global movement (Mies and Reddock 1982; Brenner and Holstrom 1983; Maguire 1984; Sen and Grown 1985).[6] Centralized, hierarchical and disciplinary structures are carefully being avoided. There is an emphasis on individual and cultural specificity. These networks can be seen as an example of Foucault's alternative power mechanisms.

The early Chilean women's movement

Having set out the similarities between Foucault's analysis of power and feminist elaborations on similar themes, the next step is to look at the Chilean women's movement.[7] First, I shall describe women's civil and political rights in Chile, the creation of groups and organizations and the specific issues put forward by them, and women's relationship with official politics, in particular with the political parties on the left. After this, these factors will be related to Foucault's analysis of the interrelatedness of the theory of sovereignty and the gender discourse, of Marxism and the creation of new forms of power.

Although Chilean women did not begin to organize themselves until the twentieth century, their awareness of existing inequalities started much earlier. The political Constitution of 1833 (Chile's second) states that all Chileans have the right to vote. However, it was not until some 50 years later that women took their case to the courts. Here it was finally admitted that the term 'Chilenos', as used in the Constitution, was in effect not a generic one, but referred only to Chilean men: women could not vote as they were not even included in the electoral registers (Covarrubias 1978: 5).

In addition to a lack of political rights, women had to face other legal problems as well. Married women – the vast majority of the adult female population – were almost entirely dependent on their husbands. They had no legal rights to their children, their property or their bodies. It was not considered a crime for a husband to kill his wife, if he caught her in the act of adultery (Covarrubias 1978: 3). The legal residence of a married woman was her husband's house and she had to get his permission to work outside the home.[8]

The development of formal education provided women with the first opportunity to leave their homes, at least for a short period in their lives, starting a process of consciousness-raising about their condition. When the law of 1860 on public education made free education available to 'all', a differentiation was made in the curriculum for boys and for girls. While boys were obliged to study the political constitution, girls had to take home economics. When the University of Chile became the first in the Americas to admit women in 1887, girls had to study in boys' secondary schools in order to meet the requirements.

Around the turn of the century, the number of working women also increased. By 1907, they made up 31 per cent of the labor force (Covarrubias 1978: 6). Access to education and work are probably the factors that contributed most to the increasing awareness of existing inequalities and to a growing need for women to get together, share their experiences and act upon them. The first women's groups emerged almost simultaneously among working-class women in the north of Chile and middle and upper-class women in the capital Santiago.

The *Centros Belén de Zarraga* were created in 1913 in the northern towns of Iquique and Antofagasta and in the adjacent saltpeter mining region in the Atacama desert. The participants were mainly the wives of the mine-workers, organized within the first Chilean socialist party, the *Partido Obrero Socialista*, by Luís Emilio Recabarren in 1912 (Kirkwood 1990: 106). Recabarren had a vivid interest in the 'woman question'. He linked the oppression of women and workers. His ideas were shared by Belén de Zarraga, an anticlerical anarchist, who became the driving force behind the women in the mining towns and helped organize conferences and demonstrations denouncing the oppression of women. They argued that it was more difficult for women than for workers to become aware of their oppression and that the role women occupy in the family should not simply be taken for granted. Although Recabarren was supportive, his aid also helped obfuscate conceptual distinctions between workers' and women's issues. Ever since this period, the interest of the Chilean left in the 'woman question' has varied depending on their electoral needs. Women have felt obliged to receive any interest with gratitude without trying to develop their own demands.

In 1915, the teacher and writer Amanda Labarca founded a *Círculo de Lectura de Señoras* in Santiago, where middle-class women met to study literary and philosophical works (Chaney 1979; Kirkwood 1990). One of their principal demands was the right of women to become integrated into the cultural life of the nation. At the end of the same year, the *Club de Señoras* was formed. These were Catholic upper-class women concerned with the fact that many middle-class women were receiving better education than they.

To our great surprise, there appeared in Chile a middle class, and we had no idea how it came to be born . . . with the most perfectly educated women who had professional and teaching degrees, while we upper class women hardly knew the mysteries of the rosary. (member of the *Club de Señoras*, quoted in Chaney 1979: 74)

Faced with their own uselessness and ignorance, their aim became to educate themselves in order to become better mothers. They emphasized the universality of women's problems and the moral superiority of women, separating them from men and male-dominated politics. Women were considered to be spiritually and morally superior to men, and political parties were thought to be corrupt and unworthy of women's attention. The *Club de Señoras* thus became the cradle for a moral feminism,[9] which was to influence liberal and conservative women's organizations until the present day. Thus, while the first working-class women's groups felt that their cause was, at least in part, taken care of by leftist parties, the first middle- and upper-class groups separated themselves from male politics altogether.

In 1919, the first women's party was created, the *Partido Cívico Femenino*, with the following main objectives: political and civil rights for women; the denunciation of fascism; religious and political independence; solidarity with working-class women and their right to unionize; access to work and education; and feminine purity. The emphasis on morality in the party was so great that it seemed to be its principal *raison d'être*, more important even than the struggle for equal rights. Since women did not have the right to vote, the party was not taken seriously by the established male-dominated parties. In the years that followed, several women's groups emerged, all emphasizing political and civil rights for women. In 1931, Chilean women finally gained the right to vote at the municipal level.

The next two decades were characterized by a worldwide economic and political crisis, which had a profound influence on the Chilean situation. As the middle classes and a growing working class became important political factors, the traditional conservative and liberal parties lost their hegemony. The membership of the recently formed communist (1922) and socialist (1933) parties (successors of the *Partido Obrero Socialista*) grew considerably. These parties joined forces in 1936 in the *Frente Popular*, the forerunner of Allende's *Unidad Popular*.

It is against this background that we should look at the

creation of the MEMCH (*Movimiento pro Emancipación de la Mujer Chilena*) in 1935, which was founded by a group of left-wing professionals, working-class women and house-wives.[10] Several thousand women became members. They were basically concerned with socialism, pointing out that when women participated in the first municipal elections only 20 per cent voted for the left.[11] The MEMCH emphasized its independence from the political parties but at the same time it advocated a double allegiance. It had a much more activist and militant character than any of the other groups and organizations had or, indeed, would ever have. Women of several social classes and political tendencies participated. It was a national organization with different types of membership at the level of villages, towns and regions. Its main goals were full political and civil rights; defence of democracy and peace; better access to culture for women and better education for children; protection of pregnant women and small children; and an increase in the standard of living of working-class women. The MEMCH also pleaded for legal divorce, access to birth control and the right to abortion (Chuchryk 1984: 261–263).

During the next decade several smaller groups were formed, all of which focused, once again, on female suffrage. These activities culminated in the first National Women's Congress in 1944, in which some 200 cultural, political, professional and religious women's organizations participated. Here the FEFICH (*Federación Chilena de Instituciones Femeninas*) was created. This collective effort of all women's organizations ultimately resulted in the attainment of the right to vote in parliamentary and presidential elections in 1949.

At this point, the relationship between women and politics began to change. In 1946 a second party had been created, the PFCh (*Partido Femenino Chileno*), which had the same principles as its predecessor the PCF. Their president was María de la Cruz, a woman with a strong personality.

Under her able leadership, the membership of the party increased to as many as 60,000 (Meza 1985: 44, 67).

After women gained the vote in 1949, the PFCh supported the conservative presidential candidate Carlos Ibañez, who advocated an authoritarian populism. He actually preached the same moral principles as the women's parties had proclaimed all along and was as opposed to 'dirty' party politics as were the women. Ibañez won the elections of 1953. The PFCh was rewarded with the post of Minister of Education (Chuchryk 1984: 270). De la Cruz recommended a woman who had no strong commitment to the goals of the party. She herself ran for the senatorial seat of the city of Santiago left vacant by Ibañez, and won. However, the election procedures antagonized the members of the PFCh, as well as left- and right-wing political parties, who were getting worried about the successes of the PFCh. The party came under attack from all directions, culminating in a formal accusation against María de la Cruz on charges of illegal importation of watches. Although a parliamentary investigation commission ruled the charges unfounded, she withdrew from parliament (Kirkwood 1990: 170). This incident divided the party even further and it was disbanded that same year. Women concluded that they were not prepared to participate in official politics. As Kirkwood says, they were trapped in their own morality and feminine purity (Kirkwood 1990: 170).

Both the MEMCH and FEFICH disappeared at about the same time. From then onward, women were only militant in the established male parties and/or participated in groups set up for women by the parties. Autonomous women's organizations were not to be seen for the next 25 years.

A new women's movement only emerged at the end of the 1970s, after several years of dictatorship. It came in the form of various women's groups and organizations with relative autonomy from the state and the political parties. The emergence of this new movement cannot be explained by a change in the relationship of the state and women. Nor were the interests of the right and the left in women as supporters of their political projects different. However, one new element was present, namely the growing awareness among many Chilean women of gender sub-ordination as a system of power relations in its own right. Some of these groups and organizations propose that the very act of organizing women around the system of gender subordination may be the unifying factor necessary to consolidate the movement, to prevent its once again slipping away under the pressure of the discourses of 'law and order' and of Marxism.

A Foucaultian perspective on the women's movement in Chile

If we try to understand what happened in the first part of this century in terms of Foucault's thinking about the interrelatedness between sovereign and disciplinary power, we can make the following tentative analysis. Women in Chile, like everywhere else, have been misled by a legal code and a Constitution, which seemingly gave them the same rights as men. Although the 1833 Constitution determined that all Chileans were equal and had the right to vote, women themselves had to point out that they could not vote as they were not even registered as voters. While Chile was the first Latin American country to adopt in 1860 a system of free public education, the curriculum for girls was quite different from that for boys and it prevented women from entering higher education. While single women had the same rights as men under civil law, this 'equality' became meaningless, since almost all women were married.

In Foucault's words: it is a fantasy to think that such a legal code is based on the 'universality of wills' (Foucault 1980: 105). The system not only conceals the intrinsic inequality ('all Chileans' = men) inherent in the law, but it embraces other mechanisms of domination, in particular gender subordination. Closely interwoven with the principle of sovereignty, these laws were made by men to be useful to men. This becomes clear when we see what happened to the first women who tried to break through the great fantasy of equality.

From a historical perspective, it seems hard to believe, for instance, that in a country with a female student population of 46 per cent in 1970 – one of the highest percentages in the world (Chuchryk 1984: 188) – less than a century earlier, women were subject to physical attack when trying to receive a proper education: '*A una señorita que estudiaba en un Instituto, los muchachos la apedriaban, gritándole: "la estudianta, la estudianta", porque era la únicamujer que asistía a los cursos*' (Vial, quoted in Kirkwood 1990: 95).[12] Even when women acted upon the rights given to them by law, as in this case, they were met by violence in the public sphere and, most likely, in the private one as well. The interdict was in the case of the schoolgirl no longer the law or rule, but the norm, materialized in the stone thrown at the girl, her experience of shame, a conflict with her parents or any other reactions to her now 'legal' rebellion. Norms based on gender ideology dictated that girls could not go to boys' schools and this must have held most girls back.

Such disciplinary mechanisms can only be perceived and studied in the materiality of everyday life. They are difficult to discover and conceptualize precisely because they are normative and take place in the isolation of private homes: 'An oppression so private would turn out hard to uproot' (Zinn 1980: 102). In Chile covering-up mechanisms took place on two distinct, but connected levels: within the legal system and in the private sphere. When Chilean women became conscious of the first level through their education and work participation, they began to struggle for legal equality and equal rights in their organizations. This struggle culminated, as it did elsewhere, in the right to vote. It took them much longer, however, to be able to conceptualize the second level. As Chaney says, in agreement with Foucault: 'The women of Latin America were slow to realize that the vote would mean little without changes in the traditions and institutions of society' (Chaney 1979: 76).

Throughout the century, however, women have had constant concern with their role in the family, motherhood, birth control, abortion, divorce, women's work and education, all of which were conflated with legal issues. An increasing awareness of gender subordination in the private sphere was clearly present. Nevertheless, the connection between the two levels of domination, as understood by Foucault and the New Feminists, was not made until much later. Thus, women's political and civil rights were still quite limited, although the laws were slowly beginning to change in their favour. This can be attributed to the persistance of a system of gender ideology in men. However, there is another factor to be considered: the internalization of gender ideology by women themselves. This was illustrated most clearly in the phenomenon of moral feminism.

Moral feminism was strongest among the liberal and conservative women of the two women's parties. Women's idea that they were morally and spiritually superior to men made them turn their backs on male politics. Moral feminism, in its exaltation of the values of homelife, motherhood and feminine purity[13] actually cuts off the possibility of entering the public domain. Once women began to enter politics, they did so by reproducing the mechanisms men had created: by founding parties of their own and holding political office. The contradictions became obvious. After the considerable success of the *Partido Femenino Chileno* and the even greater personal success of María de la Cruz in becoming a senator within the male establishment, these women destroyed their own creation on moral grounds. There seems to be a clear connection between gender ideology as internalized by women and as exploited by both the men of the period and the state system as expressed in the Chilean parliamentary system. María de la Cruz was the only woman in parliament and she left quite simply because qualities like honesty and moral superiority were expected of women. Her resignation can be seen as a disciplinary act based on the discourse of gender ideology. When Chilean women had finally managed to penetrate the system of male politics and were legally allowed to do so, gender ideology caused them to back out.

If we now direct our attention to Foucault's and the feminist critique of orthodox Marxism, several observations can be made. To begin with, the Chilean case is a good illustration of the inability of Chilean Marxists to recognize gender subordination as a separate system of domination. Once again, this can be viewed from two different angles: from the perspective of the general Marxist analysis of the 'woman question' and from the viewpoint of leftist women themselves. If we use class analysis we can divide the Chilean women's movement into a leftist/popular faction (the *Centros Belén de Zarraga* and the MEMCH) and a liberal/conservative one (the *Clubs de Señoras*, the *Partido Cívico Femenino* and the *Partido Femenino de Chile*). Such an analysis, however, fails to bring out the striking similarities in what all of these women stood for: independence from political parties; anti-clericalism; internationalism; an emphasis on democracy and peace; and political and – as specified by all of them – civil rights for women: the right to vote, right to work, right to divorce, right to education and culture, protection of mother and child and protection of working-class women.

Beginning in the late 1930s, women of a left-wing stance were urged to ally themselves with the political projects of the leftist parties. At that point, Marxist parties were beginning to gain firm ground in Chile and leftist women began to enter the various women's sections, abandoning their own organizations. In doing this, they apparently took on the Marxist analysis that conflicts in society would be resolved by class struggle, with the 'woman question' solving itself simultaneously or, if not, immediately after the revolution. These women put gender issues which would unite them with more 'conservative' women second on their political agenda. This shift in interest made it increasingly difficult to strengthen a women's movement which no longer allowed for class differences.

Simultaneously, the political center and right seized the opportunity to exploit the internalization of gender ideology among the moral feminists with their concern for motherhood, morality and purity. At first, these women had turned their backs on male politics altogether. However, from the 1950s onwards, they let themselves be influenced by the conservative ideology of the Christian Democrats and a fascist *Kinder-Küche-Kirche* ideology of the right, which was to reach its height during the military dictatorship.[14] Obviously, this shows that a better understanding of the gender problem would have been advantageous to the Marxist cause. Instead of 'writing off' the considerable number of women who, from the viewpoint of class analysis, were voting conservatively, it would have been wiser to look into the reasons for these patterns.

Kirkwood offers an interesting insight into this phenomenon. She explains conservative voting patterns in terms of consistency between public and private ideology and practice. The conservative law-and-order parties are more consistent than the leftist parties, who preach revolution and change on a societal level, while at home a law-and-order philosophy reigns. Thus, conservative women sought refuge with authoritarian leaders who, after all, interpreted situations in a way familiar to them from the domestic sphere. Kirkwood's interpretation of the inconsistency between a revolutionary class discourse and authoritarian practices in male–female relations touches on Foucault's contention that there exists a lack of analysis of parallel disciplinary discourses on the part of Marxists. Kirkwood's reflections also coincide with feminists' critique of Marxism on the same issues.

A third point concerns the construction of alternative power mechanisms on the part of the Chilean women's movement in terms of strategic knowledge, autonomy and networking. The history of the women's movement demonstrates a confusing collection of issues and strategies, in the sense that no distinction was made between gender subordination and discrimination in the legal realm. Women's organizations during the first half of the century did perceive that something was basically wrong at home (as seen in their emphasis on the rights of mother and child). They (implicitly) knew that their malaise was somehow connected with male politics and religion as demonstrated by their emphasis on organizational autonomy from both. They also (implicitly) knew that they shared gender problems with other women as shown by their cross-class positions and their internationalism. Nevertheless, their first actions were concerned with equal rights at a legal level. They were not yet able to see that their oppression in the private sphere escaped legal or state regulation. An emerging awareness of this oppression, based on the concrete everyday experience of women, could be identified as the incipience of a strategic knowledge in Foucaultian terms.

The enormous capacity to create women's groups and organizations, emphasizing autonomy from existing male-dominated institutions, can be perceived as the dawning of a new form of power through networking. By mid-century, time seemed to be ripe to integrate these new strategies and knowledge into a large women's movement, which would allow for the reversal of Chilean women's understanding of the meaning and content of power. However, once again, they chose to reinforce their relationship with the state and the political parties.

Conclusion

Foucault's analysis is useful for looking at a phenomenon like the early Chilean women's movement and its relationship to the state and political parties. His distinction between sovereign power and parallel power relations based on disciplinary discourses makes it possible to see gender ideology as a disciplinary discourse which involves power relations.

In the preceding pages I have shown how laws (= the discourse of right), from which the Chilean political institutions derive their authority, are unwittingly discriminating against women, while simultaneously, the gender discourse submits women to power relations within the private sphere. This explains why Chilean women at first struggled for legal equality. Not having the benefit of history, as we do, they could not know that achieving a right such as female suffrage would not change much in the materiality of their daily lives, even though it straightened out legal aspects. However, the equal rights struggle probably prepared the ground for that awareness, which surfaced many years later.

It is important to emphasize that the gender discourse is being internalized by both men and women. As we saw in the Chilean case, this internalization was stronger among women on the right than on the left.[15] This has an important political connotation. It may indicate that left-wing women in Chile have a greater potentiality to become aware of their internalization of the gender discourse and act upon it. At the same time, however, they are more prone, as we saw, to give preference to Marxist preoccupations. At the end of the period under consideration in this chapter both moral and left-wing feminists had entered a dead-end street, as far as their movement was concerned.

Recent developments in Eastern Europe indicate that Foucault's critique of the repetition of mechanisms of domination in excessive state bureaucracy may become obsolete in the forseeable future. However, his analysis of Marxists' failure to recognize the existence of parallel disciplinary discourses stays intact. It is needless to stress the importance of the recognition of the gender discourse as a parallel power discourse on the part of the Chilean left.

Perhaps the most interesting idea we can take from Foucault's analysis is his contention that no profound changes will take place in society unless the power mechanisms that run parallel to sovereign power (such as gender relations) are changed as well. This line of thought establishes a direct connection between gender relations and power, as operating at the level of the state. As such it explains the problematic relationship among Chilean women, the state and the political parties. Because of the internalization of the gender discourse, it is difficult for women to grasp this connection.

Unless women are able to recognize gender ideology as a power discourse in its own right, which runs parallel to state power, they will over and over again let themselves be seduced to participate in organizations and institutions which, by definition, will not address unequal gender relations. Foucault's elaborations on alternative power mechanisms, in the sense of the creation of strategic knowledge and the construction of autonomous power networks, is still a utopia in Chile, as it is elsewhere.

Nevertheless, there was a constant effort, be it unconsciously, to create such networks during the first half of the century. In that period, Chilean women built a large and influential movement. A considerable number of women from different social backgrounds were participating and a large variety of organizational forms, activities and issues became involved. Nevertheless, the movement did not persist. The women themselves did not seem to be sufficiently aware of the power they had been engendering.

To summarize, Foucault's analysis of sovereign and disciplinary power, his critique of Marxism and his ideas about power networks can be linked to feminist theory and practice and to the actual Chilean situation. By establishing this link, we can show how Foucault's analysis, even though he ignores gender issues (a form of his male bias), can shed light on the importance of the gender discourse in the turbulent relationship of women with state power and official politics.

Notes

1 Although women played a major role in the protest actions and the opposition to the Pinochet regime in general between 1973 and December 1989, when presidential and parliamentary elections were held, they were represented very poorly in the new democratic government that took office in March 1990. Only three out of 48 senators currently are women and seven of the 120 members of the chamber of deputies. There are no women ministers and only three female vice-ministers. Similar percentages can be observed in the key positions of the political parties, as well as at the level of provincial and municipal government posts.

2 Some of Foucault's reflections on the issue of power can be found in *Power/Knowledge: Selected Interviews and other Writings, 1972–1977*, edited by Colin Gordon in 1980. My analysis is based entirely on this publication.

3 This first aspect demonstrates the line of thought developed by Foucault in *Power/Knowledge*, chapter 5, 'Two Lectures'. Lecture Two: 14 January 1976: 92–108.

4 See, for example, the situation in Cuba, Nicaragua, Algeria, Ethiopia and Vietnam in Rowbotham (1972) and Mies and Reddock (1982). The situations in these countries show that a socialist victory over colonialism and imperialism does not guarantee a solution of the 'woman question'.

5 A smiliar proposal is made by the Maoists. However, Marxist praxis has shown that, in general, the discourse has overruled practice.

6 Since the beginning of the 1980s networking has become an essential strategy in the Latin American women's movement.

7 For the historical data in this chapter, I have relied heavily on Julieta Kirkwood's book *Ser política en Chile: los nudos de la sabiduría feminista* (1990) and an article by Paz Covarrubias: 'El Movimiento Feminista Chileno' (1978). Kirkwood's book is mainly the result of her own pioneering historical research done in the late 1970s and early 1980s,

before her premature death in April 1985. The other sources I use are Mattelart (1975), Chaney (1979) and Chuchryk (1984). These non-Chilean researchers have produced excellent work on women in Chile.

8   Most of these discriminatory laws are part of the latest Constitution drafted by the military regime in 1980 (see Medina 1985).

9   The term 'moral feminism' is used by Kirkwood. It is perhaps interesting to note that she was not acquainted with the concept of 'Marianismo' as developed by E. Stevens (1973) and widely used by American and European researchers. 'Marianismo' refers to the same phenomenon as 'moral feminism'.

10   For a recent interview with one of the founders of the MEMCH, see Meza (1985): 'Pioneras de una Lucha que renace. Elena Caffarena y Olga Poblete', pp. 47–73.

11   Chilean women have consistently voted conservatively. The left had its highest percentage of female voters (30.5 per cent) in the 1970 elections, when Allende won (Chaney 1979: 96; Mattelart 1975: 16). In a 1980 referendum, 75 per cent of women voted for Pinochet.

12   The translation is as follows: 'Boys threw stones at a young lady who studied in an "institute" [secondary school], shouting at her "the student, the student", [estudianta in Spanish is female], because she was the only woman that attended the classes.'

13   It is interesting to look at the way Chaney (1979) develops the concept of 'Supermadre', which touches on the same issues.

14   It is a well-known fact that women had an active role in the overthrow of the Allende government. A well-organized women's group, El Poder Femenino or Women's Power (see Mattelart 1975; Crummett 1977) – of which the ex-senator María de la Cruz was a part – arranged a series of major women's mobilizations against the government in 1972 and 1973. These women were organized in the Secretaría Nacional de la Mujer, directed by Pinochet's wife Lucía Hiriart until the changes of government in March 1990. She also leads the Centros de Madres, of which some 230,000 Chilean women were members by 1983 (Lechner and Levy 1984). These two organizations were the expression of the enormous importance given by the Pinochet government to the 'woman question'. Although the Centros de Madres have traditionally been headed by the wife of the Chilean president, a special decree, formulated just before the transfer of power, determines that, from now on, the centers will be led by the wife of the chief commander of the army. Since Pinochet stipulated, in another decree, that he will stay on as the chief commander, his wife Lucía took the centers with her, as if the members of the centers were her private property.

15 This was recently confirmed to me when, during the 1989 election campaign, I participated in meetings where women candidates of the center right political party *Renovación Nacional*, the main opposition party in the new government, exposed their viewpoints. They invariably insisted on motherhood as the central force in women's lives, on the 'natural' differences between men and women, on women's superior intuition and sensitivity and on women's different view of the world.

Bourdieu, Power and Resistance: Gender Transformation in Sri Lanka

CARLA RISSEEUW

> It is because subjects do not, strictly speaking, know
> what they are doing that what they do has more
> meaning than they know. (Bourdieu 1977: 72)

Gender transformation is a process involving subtle
changes in gender relationships, taking place over long
stretches of time, often remaining relatively unnoticed. I
use this term to describe what happened to women during
the British colonial era of Sri Lanka. The power processes I
found seemed to lack overt force, but they nevertheless,
over a period of a century or more, caused women to lose
access to crucial resources (land, labour, trade) and
decision-making in their families. Family and marriage
relations seemed to have changed, affecting not only the
degree of control over resources, but also the emotional
content of these relationships.

The subtlety of the process, which so seldom involved
open conflict and even seemed to involve a relative lack of
awareness on the part of the actors, led me to scrutinize
current theories on power and their ability to explain such
processes. In this chapter I shall explore parts of the theory
of Bourdieu in an attempt to shed light on some aspects of
the operation of power.

Due to the tradition in the social sciences of looking at
power as an empirical fact (Weber, Baratz and Bachrach,

and, to a lesser extent, Lukes), it was – until recently – even problematic to relate this kind of process to the concept of power. Following the Weberian tradition, the concept of power has been treated as a phenomenon of willed or intended action (observable and concrete), used to achieve a desired or specific outcome. Power has been projected against a background of conflict, in which one party dominates. In the Marxist tradition, power relations were analyzed as a process rather than as empirical fact. The focus on economic organization of society, class struggle and state control, however, has led to a neglect of those relations which do not seem to have a direct link with the economic base in Marxist theorizing. Neither of these approaches seemed to offer an appropriate theoretical framework for understanding the subtlety of the processes I had to deal with.

In this chapter I will address some questions concerning the conceptualization of the process of gender transformation in Sri Lanka. How does this imperceptible process operate in the specific historical context of Sri Lanka? Of theoretical frameworks that deal with power, which seems most fruitful for understanding such processes? In what respects would this framework demand further refinement or even different theoretical approaches and concepts?

Colonial influence on the position of women

The British rule of Sri Lanka established a colonial state, free enterprise, a commercial land policy and attempted to break feudal control by alienating vast tracts of land on behalf of European capitalists and their coffee, tea and rubber plantations (Snodgrass 1966; Roberts 1975b; Abeysekera 1985). In the non-plantation areas, substantial opportunity was given to wealthier Sinhalese to acquire land from others, a process which deeply disrupted the traditional forms of shared land ownership (Obeyesekera

1967). This second process, of not only taking land out of Sinhalese hands, but of redistributing it on a totally new basis of individual ownership and monetary purchase, led to a growing degree of economic mobility and subsequent struggle between the land-owning classes and their newly emerging counterparts. Exponents of the newly emerging and the land-owning classes of their time embarked on a tremendous struggle, in which every financial mistake was dearly paid for. A misguided marriage alliance could inhibit absorption into the sought-after elite (Peebles 1973; Roberts 1975b).

The debates on the nature of the change that took place have not ended. However, it is striking that the transformation in marriage and family arrangements usually goes unnoticed or, at least, remains unintegrated in analyses of the transformations which Sri Lanka underwent in this period. The marriage arrangements prior to the British era, which are now often forgotten, accorded a woman a degree of access to and control over land and property, which she was to lose imperceptibly over a period of a century or more as the colonial ruler introduced changes in the marriage and inheritance system. Local marriages included fraternal polyandry; the practice of infanticide; polygamy and group marriage (Knox 1911: 162–179). This, plus the observation that people often entered four or five marriage unions during a lifetime, gave rise to horror and amazement amongst Europeans, repeatedly to be found in writings of the time (Knox 1911: 162–179). This response led European writers to overlook the importance of family bonds, which gave men and women greater economic security than that offered by a marriage itself.

In relation to residence and property arrangements, two forms of marriage were recognized: the virilocal *Diga* in which the wife goes to and lives on her husband's land, and the uxorilocal *Binna* marriage, in which the husband lives on his wife's family land and the children take the mother's family name. In the latter case, the husband acquires no right to his in-laws' land and is liable to expulsion or divorce by the wife or her parents at any moment (Peiris 1956: 204). In this system, the phenomenon of a bastard child did not exist. All children born to a woman were accepted by her family, provided they were fathered by men of similar or higher rank/caste (Hayley 1923).[1]

One of the most important consequences for women of the traditional system was the great importance of the family as a social unit. Even after marriage, a woman could always fall back on the family of origin and in *Diga* marriages she could even regain the right to inherit family land. In *Binna* marriages, similar rights were accorded to the man within his family of origin. In practice, this meant that a woman who returned from a *Diga* marriage to her mother's or father's family would regain her right to own the land and could subsequently be married in either *Binna* or *Diga* by her family (Risseeuw 1988).

Two trends developed after the implementation of the British marriage legislation. First, the legislation worked toward a monogamous, life-long union, sanctified by state and/or church with a preference for virilocal residence and patrilineal inheritance. It reduced the number of persons for whom the older family members could be held legally responsible, by creating a category of 'bastards' and changing 'adoption' from a family decision to a legal procedure. This legislation not only operated in opposition to the traditional bilateral inheritance laws, but also attempted to introduce 'primogeniture', so that only the firstborn son would inherit. The new system, therefore, created greater inequality of access to family land and property among family members and reduced responsibility of the newly privileged, select male members, for the less privileged.

Secondly, the woman's relatively independent position in marriage, provided by her life-long access to land and property and right to divorce, shifted to that of a legal and economic dependent with limited divorce rights. She was to be protected by her husband or, upon his default, by the state. Her position became one which was, at best, secure but lacking in economic potential, because even as a widow her rights to land and property were curtailed (Hayley 1923, ch. 5).

In retrospect, each law or ordinance over a period of ten to 20 years made seemingly small changes. Taken together, however, they led to further state control over matters, which had remained totally outside the scope of the state in earlier Sri Lankan society.[2] The British usually portrayed these ordinances as 'fitting responses' to changing times, carried out under pressure to 'civilize' the population. But moral pursuits and mistaken superiority were not the only reasons for British attempts to transform marriage and register each individual birth and death in the country. In the light of the land policy mentioned above, it is obvious that the British would want to opt for a form of enduring monogamy. Economic power would preferably be limited to one spouse and networks of responsibility reduced from a large extended family to smaller units. This was a prerequisite for the successful transition to the private initiative and individual ownership they envisaged. Thus, marriage reform and privatized land ownership can be seen as the logical components of a single design. In theory, this could have been achieved by putting property in the hands of the wife instead of the husband, but the choice of the latter was too obvious to require further consideration. It is important to realize that such major modifications in the position of women could be effected, while not being consciously sought after, or even remaining relatively unnoticed among the many other changes taking place at the same time.

Sinhalese response to British marriage legislation

In the context of this chapter only a few short comments must suffice to indicate the nature of the resistance to the British legislation. Initially, the marriage legislation was ignored, especially among the rural population. Shifts taking place in land ownership, however, finally caught up with people's lives and the decisions being taken by families. In an upsurge of property disputes, family members began falling back on either the traditional laws or on the often contradictory opportunities offered by British legislation (Sess. P. no. 3, 17, 1869). The role of women in these conflicts was sometimes acknowledged, but the structural change in their position within the family was rarely noted (Sess. P. no. 4, 26, 1869).

Change did not become apparent through recorded conflict alone. At a conceptual level, women were slowly 'discussed out' of the system. In this process, exponents of the Sinhalese male elite, serving as informants to the British administrators, influenced British perception in accordance with their own interests: the reduction of female rights to inheritance.

The confusing information the British received, for example, facilitated, on paper, the transformation of the concept 'widow'. In a Sinhalese version a widow could have substantial inheritance rights and the ability to, under certain circumstances, transfer inherited property into another family upon marriage. In the British concept a widow received maintenance and had a life interest in land and property only as a guardian of her children (Hayley 1923: 352).

A second example is found in the British analysis implying a higher and increasing frequency of *Diga* over *Binna* marriages. The second form was presented subsequently as an aberration of the former. Again this can be related to the interests of the Sinhalese informants as, due to the British legislation, a *Binna* marriage was to become less attractive than formerly. Such a marriage might have been a temporal union due to relative poverty. A man and his relations had to enter such a union on a much more permanent base, however, after the intervention of the British, demanding life-lasting monogamy.

In a third instance, exponents of the Sinhalese male elite came close to openly attempting to reduce their women's access to family resources. In the 1850s, the Governor twice received a petition requesting marriage customs to be adjusted to the more appropriate British model (Roberts 1975a: 29). Reading between the lines, the petition was a thinly disguised assault on the independent position of a married daughter who, in the case of divorce, 'traditionally' had the right to return to her family of origin and claim her share of land and property. The British realized that the petitions, although claiming to speak for the whole population, were the voice of the privileged alone. Nevertheless, they seized the occasion and implemented the ordinance required (1859; Roberts 1975a: 31).

On the surface, argument on both sides was couched in terms of 'elevating' and 'purifying' the Sinhalese institution of marriage. The underlying reasons and their connection to the drastic economic changes taking place in the country would have been interpreted differently by the British and the Sinhalese. The interesting point is, that such a change could lead to a reduction in women's access to resources and loss of their independent position in marriage and family arrangements, without any open consideration of these facts by either party.[3]

Implications of gender transformation

We have seen how changes in marriage legislation appeared to be unconnected to land ownership, which was crucial to the struggle to take part in the new social mobility. Due to the length of time involved, each successive ordinance seemed no more than an obvious next step, based on a shared common sense. Articulation of this conflict of interests on a political level was, therefore, absent.

During the latter half of the nineteenth century and the first half of the twentieth, paid labour and trade grew in importance for the Sinhalese population, due to the progressive breakdown of the feudal network and increasing land scarcity (Sarkar 1957). Here, a similar process occurred. Although women shared in the necessity of having to find work or undertake petty trade, they slowly found themselves in the least advantageous sectors of new avenues of income. They lost their traditional work or trade activities, which had formerly proved quite profitable. They had no access to the highest paying jobs created by the colonizer – lawyer, doctor or civil servant – and, of course, they had no individual rights to land, in the land schemes created to alleviate the worst effects of growing landlessness (Land Development Ordinance, 1935; Sess. P. no. 18, 1929).

This process did not require an articulation on a policy level, either. In the various censuses preceding the process, the definition and contribution of the 'female worker' had already become blurred, making it easy for policy-makers to ignore what was taking place with regard to women (for further elaboration, see Risseeuw 1988, ch. 2). Individual protests by women supported by their relatives can be found in series of petitions and recordings by government agents. The upsurge in crime and lawsuits concerning the division of family land and divorce, in which women also took part, indicate the severe social and economic upheaval experienced by the population.

The process described above, which I call gender transformation, spanned a period of at least 150 years and had effects on different levels:

1 On a material level, women, depending on their class,

lost ground on land, labour and trade resources *vis-à-vis* their men and could not take advantage of newly created avenues of income.

2 On a conceptual level, terms like 'husband', 'wife', 'widow', 'land', 'family', as well as newly created terms like 'female worker', took on new meanings in relation to one another.

3 On both levels, changes began to take on a life of their own as men and women found themselves in new positions *vis-à-vis* one another, both in society at large and at the level of the family and interpersonal relationships. In time, this altered the emotional content of family bonds and the number of people to whom various kinds of responsibility were owed.

Imagining oneself in the position of a woman in a polyandric or *Binna* union will suffice to realize how different her outlook on human relations and, more specifically, family relations must have been from that of a woman married in a monogamous, life-long *Diga* marriage, living among her in-laws. Her whole perception of her worth to her own relations and her children, as well as her position toward her husband's relations, would have had a radically different emotional content. In the former case, as a mother she possessed active economic power to protect and influence the lives of her children. In the latter, her relationship with her children would depend largely on 'love' and 'affection', as she could do little more than manipulate or influence their father and his relations on their behalf. They would, therefore, have regarded her in a fundamentally different light. Similarly, the man's position would have been influenced by the two different marriage systems.

  In both cases, women and men are likely to have had totally different perceptions of themselves and each other and have created an entirely different process of socialization with regard to their children. Children would gradually grow up with transformed interpretations of what women and men can do and be in the family and society at large. The ideal of woman- and man-hood would also be altered and different requirements would be imposed on the behaviour of both sexes. These changing interpretations of gender would, in turn, create new platforms of common sense. Though unarticulated, this played a subtle role in how new economic realities would be conceived and responded to.

Gender transformation and the theory of Bourdieu

In this section, I will attempt to address some of the questions raised by the case study described above. Can actors be assumed to have been conscious of the implications of their actions? This question can be posed with regard to different categories of actors: the British administrators, the Sinhalese male elite in contact with them and the Sinhalese women within their families. The dichotomy itself, between conscious and unconscious, seemed to inhibit further understanding of the processes involved. Questions remained, also, concerning the relative lack of overt resistance and conflict in relation to the gender transformation described. I found myself in need of a framework to understand power processes operating from a basis of consensus, or rather 'acquiescence'. The latter concept might be more apt as it refers to 'submission with apparent consent or a disposition to submit or yield. It includes (apparently) satisfied passivity or the lack of opposition; discontentment, usually after previous opposition; uneasiness or dislike, but with ultimate compliance and submission' (McKechnie 1971).

In the context of this chapter I will attempt to deal with these questions mainly in relation to concepts developed by Bourdieu in his work *Towards a Theory of Practice* (1977). In criticizing a dominant theoretical approach of his time, structuralism, Bourdieu attempts to come to terms with what he calls the dilemma of determinism and freedom. He discusses the limits of structuralist analysis, stating that the major concepts developed, 'structures' and 'model', misrepresent the full process taking place at the agent level. Bourdieu maintains that the truth of an interaction between people can never be fully contained within the interaction; nor can it be fully determined by the 'structure' or 'model' developed by the anthropologist. He attempts to create an opening which enables moments of action to be located even in the most ritualistic exchanges, allowing scope for response or 'strategies' over which the agents retain some degree of command. Bourdieu proposes that agents are not fully aware of their own conduct and operate from what he terms 'learned ignorance': a mode of practical knowledge which does not include knowledge of its own principles. From this perspective, the advantage of the term 'acquiescence' over that of 'consensus' also becomes clear. The former term allows more room for decisions which did not seem to be decisions at the time they were made.

One of Bourdieu's most important ways of combating the false dichotomy between structure and practice is his mediating concept of 'habitus'. Habitus becomes a 'way of being', something between a conscious strategy and a disposition. It indicates 'those series of moves which are objectively organized as strategies without being the product of genuine intention' (Bourdieu 1977: 73) or a 'system of dispositions', an endless capacity to

> engender products, thoughts, perceptions, expressions, actions, whose limits are set by the historically and socially situated conditions of its production . . . it gives an agent a sense of limits in the widest sense of the term, while it also offers a legitimate transgression of limits, on the basis of knowing and ordering of the

world and strategies of handling necessary or
unavoidable breaches of that order. (Bourdieu 1977:
124)

From her or his earliest upbringing, each individual is
consciously engaged in mastering this common code
through confrontations with other individuals. By definition, it also presupposes a minimum concordance in the
worldviews of interacting agents. By coining habitus as an
area between that of 'willed intention' and a 'disposition'
located inside and outside the agents themselves, Bourdieu
has opened a subtle region of decision-making in and
interaction between people, which is relevant for the study
of gender relationships. This makes it possible to analyze
how 'dispositions' – even if they are not consciously
formulated – can play a crucial role in determining what
will seem to an agent as 'the widest sense of limits' within
which he or she can act or think.

From his concepts of habitus, Bourdieu develops what he
calls a series of 'strategies', which are operationalized to a
greater degree than the diffuse and abstract concept of
habitus. This opens the way to a better understanding of
the 'limited freedom' he accords individuals. Strategies can
also be used to analyze how a process of change takes
shape.

In his explanation of the concept of strategies, Bourdieu
uses the concept of 'gift', taken from the work of Mauss, as
an example. In addition to a mechanical sequence of
obligatory acts, gift and the counter-gift can be interpreted
as a series of 'at once risky and necessary improvisations of
everyday strategies' (Bourdieu 1977: 171). The giver's
undeclared calculation must reckon with the receiver's
undeclared recognition, attempting to satisfy her/his
expectations without appearing to know what they are.
The most profitable strategies are those which give the
illusion of the 'most authentic' sincerity, leading to the
seeming disinterestedness with which gift-giving is carried

out. Strategies might operate in the field of education, fertility, matrimony etc.

Bourdieu applies his concept of strategies to various levels of interaction between agents. Strategies include the context of family life and gender relationships, permitting a social relationship like marriage to be seen as an organization of opposing interests. In the context of nineteenth-century Sri Lanka, we can use the concept of strategies hypothetically, particularly the most profitable (i.e. the seemingly authentic ones), to reconstruct the decision-making in the Sinhalese families faced with new avenues of mobility and commercial land ownership. It becomes clear how convenient it is for the 'head' of a family or the leader of a group to merge the interests of all with his own interests. Thus, a male head of a family would seldom have faced much opposition from other (female) members, if he promoted certain decisions on behalf of his family in response to the pressure of the British colonial policy which, at the same time, incorporated his own interests. In many cases, his wife may have 'acquiesced'. If she did not, he was in a strong position to discredit her attitude. Similarly, if both spouses were running separate small business enterprises, capital to expand might well have been available only for the husband. Since his property had become equated with the property of all and his freedom in society at large was greater, he would have seemed the more suitable of the two to receive support. In this case, the wife would have acquiesced to, what would have appeared to her, as well as the other family members, as the most sensible, appropriate decision to take. In many instances, it would not have been a question of a husband's conscious decision to overrule his wife's access to the family's resources. Decisions would be guided more by 'implicit principles', defying articulation not because they were necessarily taken unconsciously, but rather because they required no further questioning. In this subtle area of the habitus of decision-making within the family, the interests of the weaker family members would dissolve as their assertion would be linked to a weakening or destruction of the family's interests as a whole. In addition to Bourdieu's concept of habitus, the emphasis on 'time' as a gift can be an explosive approach if applied to gender. Women often give their time, not only to their husbands and children, but also to relatives, acquaintances and those who form part of the 'network of alliances' on whom a family can depend. Especially within family relationships, this gift is not without returns in the form of bonds of love, protection and dependence. Nevertheless, if the expected amount of time given remains the same or increases while access to resources decreases, one's position becomes progressively more insecure. Furthermore, if one's position in a network of people (e.g. a family) becomes increasingly defined in terms of 'time' rather than as a degree of resource control, one's position shrinks at a conceptual level as well. Returning to our Sri Lankan example, it must have been very different for children facing financial difficulties, to turn to a mother able to give only love and consolation, than to one who also had access to her own property, and could offer concrete help through her influence on their inheritance.

Another series of Bourdieu's concepts which are illuminating when used from a feminist perspective are those of 'orthodoxy', 'heterodoxy' and 'doxa'. These concepts are concerned with possibilities and strategies involved in effecting degrees of social change and they distinguish different levels of adherence to the social order. 'Doxa' indicates the consensus: 'self-evidence of the common sense world' (Bourdieu 1977: 167). Tradition is silent about itself, unaware of the question of legitimacy which might be leveled at it and arbitrary in the most absolute sense of the word. This includes, for example, classification systems based on sex, age and position in relations of production. Each system makes its specific contribution to the reproduction of the power relations of which it is a product. The political function of classification passes unnoticed all the more easily if the prevailing classificatory system encounters no rival or antagonistic principles. In domestic conflicts, categories of agents disadvantaged by the symbolic order, like women and children, often have no option, other than recognizing the legitimacy of the dominant classification, because actually this is their only chance to neutralize effects which would be quite opposed to their interests.

In contrast, 'orthodoxy' represents the 'dominant articulated opinion'. This is a manifest form of censorship which imposes an opposition between 'right' and 'wrong' opinion and limits the 'universe of possible discourse' by attempting – without ever fully succeeding – to restore the primal state of the innocence of doxa. 'Heterodoxy' represents articulated discourse as opposition, which is, nevertheless, also determined by doxa, again setting the limits of its logic (Figure 7.1).

To explain these concepts, Bourdieu uses the example of class struggle, which he defines as a struggle around the imposition of the dominant systems of classification. The dominant classes have a stake in defending the integrity of doxa or, at least, in establishing orthodoxy as an imperfect substitute. On the other hand, the dominated classes have an interest in 'pushing back the limits of Doxa', thereby reducing the area of that which is beyond question. The ability and degree of success in unlocking 'what goes without saying and what cannot be said' within the limits of discourse, both orthodox and heterodox, forms the line of separation between the 'most radical form of misrecognition' and the 'awakening of political consciousness':

> Private experiences undergo nothing less than a 'change of state' when they recognize themselves in the public objectivity of an already constituted discourse, the objective sign of recognition of their right to be spoken and to be spoken publicly. (Bourdieu 1977: 170)

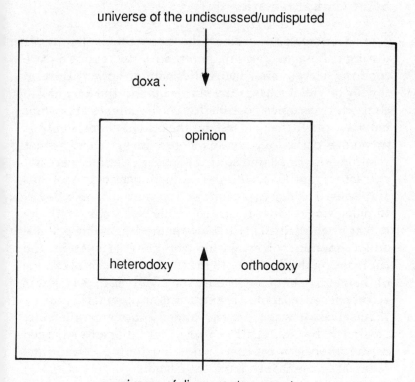

Figure 7.1   Bourdieu's concepts of orthodoxy, heterodoxy and doxa (Bourdieu 1977: 168)

The establishment of dominant classes or gender can be opposed, but they must be challenged on two levels. Order and the rule itself must be opposed, without falling into the trap of heterodox opinion alone. The challenge lies in delimiting the struggle to the terrain of doxa, of the unsaid, which forms the most powerful rule of all. Placed in the perspective of the limited freedom of the individual, these three concepts – doxa, orthodoxy and heterodoxy – are helpful tools in analyzing the described process of gender transformation as well as power relations in general.

Some critical remarks

The advantage of Bourdieu's three concepts is that, while distinguishing an opposing heterodoxy, he retains a place for doxa, a large area which defies naming both by those in favour of and opposing the status quo. In the Sri Lankan context, it becomes possible to see the interrelationships between the British rulers and the Sinhalese male elite as involving orthodoxy versus heterodoxy, while gender relations remained undisputed. Gender relations were not extracted from doxa, whereas the legitimacy of the colonial state was. The colonized elite were eventually able slowly to delegitimize British control. This was done partly by defeating the British at their own game: by gaining political and economic power within the colonial system and confronting the British with the contradictory implications of their arguments concerning state control. In part, it was accomplished by gradually extracting arguments favouring themselves. It was from the landed and mercantile elite, created in the nineteenth century, that exponents emerged in the twentieth century, who contributed to the final removal of the British from the island.

Although the gender ideologies of the British and the Sinhalese were by no means congruent, neither party had any interest in highlighting gender issues. On the contrary, the more positive points for women in the traditional system could be fairly smoothly maneuvered back into the field of the undisputed, much to the advantage of both parties. There were no rival or antagonistic principles in the Sinhalese ideology. The relative equality between men and women in family arrangements was not matched in the political or religious world; nor did the corresponding symbolism incorporate a strongly developed female orientation which might have influenced the 'widest sense of limits' and obstructed the possibility of an unnoticed transformation process in relation to gender.

Another advantage of Bourdieu's concepts is that they

neither involve a dichotomy nor do they imply a linear development, but rather a pendulum or a combination of two arguments. Counter-arguments can lose force or be pushed back into the area of the unsaid. However, Bourdieu places relatively little emphasis on analyzing what happens to 'doxa' over time. The interesting point for a feminist analysis is not only that gender relations can remain undisputed within the context of severe conflicts over land and property, but that they can be imperceptibly transformed over time as the alteration in property relations is consolidated. What would have appeared to one generation to be beyond the 'widest sense of limits' could well be considered 'normal' or 'obvious' to the next. Although people remain to a large extent unaware of it, gender relations do change in content over time and it is in this context that the term 'transformation of doxa' – although it is to my knowledge not to be found in Bourdieu's work – might be useful. For example, referring back to the Sri Lankan case, a mother married in *Binna*, polyandrous or not, will choose her strategies from the options she conceives to be open to her. As time passes and marriage changes in relation to access to resources, the new, more limited options will appear immutable, because the first transformations were not articulated. They seemingly took place for other reasons and were not recognized as power transformations between the sexes. Nevertheless, they created new identities for men and women – new forms of the 'gender of habitus' – both as individuals and in relation to each other. These provide different options, while interacting with the emerging social and economic realities.

Furthermore, any system of gender relations can be seen as involving a higher or lower degree of gender polarization. For example, gender relations became further polarized within the Sinhalese family in the sense that women lost and men gained access to resources, while the contribution of the former to the home and family focused more on the time given. It is also important to realize that it is not only women who change in a process of gender transformation. Power relations always have a dual effect, forcing those whose basis of power is increasing to transform themselves in relation to the 'other', whom they believe they must rule, oppress, protect or guide. That this process does not receive full attention in Bourdieu's work could be caused by the lack of precise definition of one of his main concepts, habitus. Critics have remarked that this concept has to explain too much and therefore too little (Di Maggio 1979; Brubaker 1985; Klaver and Onstenk 1985). It is only in his earlier work that Bourdieu distinguishes between a male and female habitus in a given culture. In *Towards a Theory of Practice*, he drops this distinction, thereby reducing the potential of a gender specific analysis.

In relation to the concept of doxa, one can also question whether the concept contains some system, some form of hierarchy. At a given point in history, the widest sense of limits enables an opposing opinion or heterodoxy to emerge, while other perspectives seem unable to surface. Thus, although the concepts around doxa offer stimulating advantages, their neatness and elegance should not inhibit one from asking further questions. The task remains to distinguish, for example, between the silence of an actor, due to an attempt to neutralize effects opposed to her/his interests, and the silence which is due to a lack of perception of the situation. The difference can be a gradual one, can shift – even back and forth – over time, and indeed 'habitus' as a concept covers both and gives room to the fluidity needed. But although the rigidity of a dichotomy should not be recreated, a conceptualization of two ends of a continuum might facilitate distinguishing between coerced and acquiesced doxa (Risseeuw 1988: ch. 3).

This is related to a last critical point which I would like to raise in the context of this chapter, concerning the conceptualization of resistance. Bourdieu's analysis of resistance stresses that the disadvantaged/oppressed within a social relation often cannot do otherwise than comply with the dominant classification, not necessarily because they have internalized it, but because compliance is the best option open to them. Thus concepts such as 'habitus' and 'strategies' make it possible to contradict views of the 'oppressed' as being too ignorant or passive to oppose forces controlling them. This analysis circumvents simplistic notions of actors lacking 'consciousness', and also gives more room to respect people's actions, as it accords others an ability to assess and judge their situation, rather than classifying them as too ignorant to do so.

Bourdieu's concept of resistance can be criticized on two points. Bourdieu emphasizes a strong utilitarian bent in the response of his 'actors'. They can be interpreted as being forever involved (un)consciously in optimizing their social positions, by acquiring cultural, social and economic capital. Bourdieu is relatively silent on the potential of a joint struggle for change, of organization and political cooperation between groups. This perspective has been criticized by a number of authors, who speak of Bourdieu's actors as strategists and not strugglers. His world contains endless transformations rather than revolutions and social change (Swartz 1977; Di Maggio 1979; Garnham and Williams 1980; Joppke 1987). This criticism is closely linked to Bourdieu's emphasis on class struggle taking place solely among the dominant groups themselves, which strive for a symbolic legitimacy of their interpretation of the world. Social change at best becomes no more than a circulation of elites. The dominated class, located by the above writers in the working class, is seen by Bourdieu as devoid of all interaction in this struggle for legitimacy: 'The proletariat is invisibly forced to be silent, or to resort to the clumsy and fragmented use of a language "borrowed" from political and cultural elites' (Joppke 1987: 68).

The problem from a feminist view is that in the Sri Lankan case described, Bourdieu's analysis, even if framed less cynically, largely covers the process as it took place. Women lost ground not so much because men were opposing them, but because men were opposing each other. Nevertheless, I disagree with Bourdieu's position that the dominated, whether working-class women or other oppressed groups, do not possess a distinct discourse, even if the prevailing ideas (orthodoxy) of an epoch are always those of the ruling class, race or gender. Furthermore, I hold the view that this distinct discourse can in principle – under certain conditions – 'burst the bourgeois hegemony' (Joppke 1987: 66). A utilitarian reductionism can overlook an existing moral core of legitimate culture, which follows an internal rationality and can run against the (un)conscious intent of the ruling class, race, gender, although these have been able to assert their worldview or orthodoxy as the dominant one (Joppke 1987).

For example, in Sri Lanka as in many colonized countries, the colonial empire was to an extent also discredited by the very values it initially upheld on the basis of its assumed superiority. Likewise in the West, feminism could emerge because former heterodoxies of socialism and communism have transformed notions of justice and equality. This normative dimension of struggle, whether tied to class, race or gender, has no place in Bourdieu's framework and therefore he does not develop a perspective of an autonomous culture/resistance among the dominated, which can lead to the formation of collective identities as their resistance gains momentum.

A second point of criticism of Bourdieu's view on resistance is that he not only underestimates its presence and potential, but also the depths of its dilemma. His model of habitus tends to lead him to overlook different dimensions of resistance, although they are implicitly present in his framework. By disregarding organized resistance and allowing no scope for opposition among the most oppressed groups in society, Bourdieu obscures the distinctions between varying levels of heterodoxy and the dimension of the psychological contract that can exist between the powerful and the weak (Nandy 1983). In other words, at times the demarcations between doxa and heterodoxy remain obscure. This refers back to the earlier point of the 'elegance' of some of Bourdieu's concepts. For example, in his analysis of the functioning of symbolic violence, Bourdieu states that both the dominant and the dominated agree to misrecognize the nature of the relationship. But the degrees in which they do this wittingly or unwittingly is neatly circumvented with the concept of habitus, as it entails both.

In a recent interview, Bourdieu did not really answer his critics in relation to the concept of resistance (Bourdieu 1989: 36–37). In spite of these critical points, however, many of his concepts can be fruitfully used and developed within a feminist framework.

Conclusion

In summary, two major areas of relevance can be inferred from my analysis. The first concerns a theory conceptualizing power and resistance. When the process of gender transformation is being analyzed, the notion of power needs a conceptual framework which allows all parties to be invested with power, thereby dissolving the dichotomy between the powerful and the powerless. It has to enable us to see how the powerful and the less powerful become transformed both in their conceptualizations of themselves as well as of the 'other' in the course of their interaction. A potential to operate without formulated conflict or without power being named must be incorporated in the theory. In such a framework, the most powerful have to be accorded the ability to operate from levels of ignorance while, at the same time, asserting their power. The less powerful, on the other hand, have to be accorded a sense of awareness of their disadvantaged position. Even if this entails non-articulation or indirect forms of resistance, it should not be equated with ignorance. A theory of power and resistance needs concepts which incorporate the vast scope of an unarticulated frame of reference, providing the final 'borders' making conceptualization possible in the first place. Finally, it has to provide an understanding of how power relationships can change in content over time as well as how they can be resisted. Without wanting to suggest that power cannot also be asserted by (the threat of) brutal and physical force, it is also important that we get a grip on the more subtle, unformulated operations of power. To this end, the theories of Bourdieu can offer a substantial contribution to developing a feminist analysis of how power and resistance operate in the context of distinctions based on gender.

The second conclusion is connected to the danger of gender transformations recurring in a manner comparable to the past, and the implications this has for the development of a feminist movement. In the Sri Lankan case, however negative and forceful the colonial impact was, it was but one incident in a series of events. Sri Lanka had several thousand years of written history prior to European colonialism and there are strong indications to support the hypothesis that similar transformations occurred in pre-colonial Sri Lanka (Risseeuw 1986: 38–39). At various points in history, Sinhalese women in Sri Lanka lost access to political and religious participation and decision-making. In the context of the symbolic order, the male principle became more pronounced, leading to a dimming of the female presence. In fact, family and marriage relationships were the only areas of society that had remained relatively 'equal' and uninfluenced before the advent of European colonialism. In retrospect, it appears that these prior transformations made the success of the British as well as the Sinhalese male elite possible (Risseeuw 198: ch. 3).

The process of gender transformation, however, can

also occur in the current age. Given the parallels in the approach of the colonial administration and that of current development policy-makers, this danger seems quite real. In both cases, the most powerful sets a discourse, divorced from the reality of gender relations and, at the same time, attempts to create and reallocate resources in society. Once more, gender and family relationships are being transformed, while policymakers do not have to address the impact of their policies and many will remain ignorant of these effects of their activities. Thus, the developmentalist policy-maker of today in many ways shares the ignorance of the colonial administrator of the past.

Similarly, a struggle concerning the reallocation of resources within society itself can emerge from this process, which can – as in the past – reduce the legitimacy of the struggle of the most oppressed. In the case of this analysis, that of the subordinate gender. The opposition to this process poses one of the greatest challenges to the feminist movement today. Unlike the past, the feminist movement now has the potential of joining individual women's voices, separated by class and race, to contribute to a shared platform entailing a greater legitimacy than individualized forms of resistance can achieve. Feminism is rapidly passing from the stage of struggling only for women's issues, to that of formulating demands for society and the content of human relations in general. The insight that power entails a two-way process, gives rise to challenges to the dominant to transform themselves, rather than to incorporate women somehow and somewhere in the orthodoxy of their thought.

In this context Bourdieu's biting analysis, however uncomfortable, is relevant; he stresses the struggle among the privileged themselves, and the relative inability of the oppressed even to enter into the 'dialogue' among more privileged groups. This situation can also be seen today, where many disadvantaged women in various parts of the world, cannot enter into a dialogue with the many planners, developmentalists, feminist or not, who are involved in activities on their behalf. Furthermore, the current researchers, activists and the like in the feminist movement often have to base their influence on qualities (of education, class, caste and race), which are accorded validity in the orthodoxy of dominant thinking. Although such tools cannot be disregarded – they provide one of the few possibilities to start transforming orthodox thinking – they also contain a certain danger, as this process can confirm Bourdieu's reserved analysis of the potential of social change. In other words, women who emerge as feminists, will have to become more than what Bourdieu's critics have termed 'optimizers' and transform themselves into 'strugglers'. Thus it becomes of crucial and central importance to build up sustained links with women lacking the orthodox privileges and create a platform of thought in which they can intervene on the level of discourse itself. Feminist theory will have to give extensive thought and dialogue to seeking creative new forms of organization and alliance with the dominated which are not facile copies of situations of class struggle, and avoid the failings of hierarchy and matronage inherent in many traditional (heterodox) organizations all over the world.

Notes

1   A child was a bastard only if a woman had mated beneath her caste, in which case her male family members (including her husband if she was married) had the right to chastise and even kill her in order to restore the dignity of the family. This practice was in conflict with the ideas of the British, who tried to curb these male rights within the family and replace them by marriage laws, under which a man could be brought to court for killing his wife.
2   Book of Ordinances, National Archives, Colombo. 1823: Ordinance no. 9 on infanticide. 1842: Ordinance no. 2 further penalties for infanticide and required registration of birth and death of infant. 1846: Ordinance no. 7 declared 'bigamy' unlawful. 1859: Ordinance no. 13 made both polygamy and polyandry penal offences and

required a ceremony as proof of marriage. 1865: non-registration of marriage could be fined. 1870: Ordinance no. 3 children born 'out of wedlock' illegitimate, divorce curtailed, alimony through courts, registration of marriage further streamlined. Further refinements to these major changes are found in ordinances no. 10 of 1896; no. 19 of 1900; no. 19 of 1907; no. 27 of 1917; no. 18 of 1923.

3 For a fuller discussion of these examples, see Risseeuw (1988) ch. 1.

Bibliography

Abeysekera C. (ed.) (1985) *Capital and Peasant Production: Studies in the Continuity and Discontinuity of Agrarian Studies in Sri Lanka*. Colombo: Social Scientists Association.

Aerts, M. (1981) 'Het raam van de studeerkamer', *Tijdschrift voor Vrouwenstudies*, 3: 360–375.

Aerts, M. (1986a) 'Gewoon hetzelfde of nu eenmaal anders: een feministisch dilemma', in: G. Boekraad et al. (eds.), *Te Elfder Ure 39: Dilemma's van het feminisme*. Nijmegen: SUN. pp. 4–13.

Aerts, M. (1986b) 'Het persoonlijke is politiek: een poging tot herdenken', in: G. Boekraad et al. (eds.), *Te Elfder Ure 39: Dilemma's van het feminisme*. Nijmegen: SUN. pp. 78–108.

Alic, M. (1982) 'The History of Women in Science: a Women's Studies Course', *Women's Studies International Forum*, 5 (1): 75–81.

Amsberg, K. and Steenhuis, A. (1982) *Denken over liefde en macht*. Amsterdam: Van Gennep.

Arms, S. (1975) *Immaculate Deception*. New York: Bantam Books.

Asch, S. (1956) 'Studies on Independence and Conformity: a Minority of One Against an Unanimous Majority', *Psychological Monographs*, 70 (9).

Atkinson, J.M. and Heritage, J. (eds.) (1983) *Structures of Social Action: Studies in Conversation Analysis*. Cambridge: Cambridge University Press.

Bachrach, P. and Baratz, M.S. (1970) *Power and Poverty: Theory and Practice*. New York: Oxford University Press.

Bernard, J. (1964) *Academic Women*. New York: Meridian Press.

Berscheid, E. (1985) 'Interpersonal Attraction', in: G. Lindzey and E. Aronson (eds.), *The Handbook of Social Psychology*. New York: Random House. pp. 413–485.

Bettelheim, B. (1977) *The Uses of Enchantment*. New York: Random House.

Blackstone, T. and Fulton, O. (1975) 'Sex Discrimination among University Teachers: a British–American Comparison', *British Journal of Sociology*, 26 (3): 261–275.

Blok, E. (1978) *Loonarbeid van vrouwen 1945–1955*. Nijmegen: SUN.

Blood, R.O. and Wolfe, D.M. (1960) *Husbands and Wives*. New York: Free Press.

Bonaparte, E. (ed.) (1982) *Women, Power and Policy*. New York: Pergamon Press.

Bonte Was (1974) *Vrouwen over seksualiteit*. Amsterdam: De Bonte Was.

Bonte Was (1976) *Het moederboek*. Amsterdam: De Bonte Was.

Books of Ordinances (1823) Ordinance no. 9; (1842) no. 2; (1846) no. 7; (1859) no. 13; (1870) no. 3; (1896) no. 10; (1900) no. 19; (1907) no. 19; (1917) no. 27; (1923) no. 18. (1935) Land Development Ordinance. National Archives: Colombo.

Boserup, E. (1970) *Women's Role in Economic Development*. New York: St Martins Press.

Bourdieu, P. (1977) *Towards a Theory of Practice*. Oxford: Oxford University Press.

Bourdieu, P. (1985) 'The Social Space and the Genesis of Groups', *Theory and Society*, 14 (6): 723–749.

Bourdieu, P. (1989) 'Social Space and Symbolic Power', *Sociological Theory*, 7 (1): 14–63.

Brenner, J. and Holstrom, N. (1983) 'Women's Self-Organization: Theory and Strategy', *Monthly Review*, 35 (4): 34–45.

Brink, G. van den (1978) 'Ideologie en hegemonie bij Gramsci', in: H.C. Boekraad and H. Hoeks (eds.), *Te Elfder Ure 24: Ideologietheorie 1*. Nijmegen: SUN. pp. 10–57.

Brubaker, R. (1985) 'Rethinking Classical Theory: The Sociological Vision of Pierre Bourdieu, *Theory and Society*, 14: 743–775.

Caplan, P. (1984) 'Cognatic Descent, Islamic Law and Women's Property on the East African Coast', in: R. Hirshon (ed.), *Women and Property, Women as Property*. New York: St Martin's Press.

Caplan, P. (1987) *The Cultural Construction of Sexuality*. London: Tavistock.

Census Reports (1870, 1884, 1890, 1901, 1911, 1921, 1930, 1946, 1971) Colombo: Department of Census and Statistics.

Chaney, E. (1979) *Supermadre: Women in Politics in Latin America*. Austin: University of Texas Press.

Chester, G. (1979) 'I Call Myself a Radical Feminist', *Practice. Notes from the Tenth Year*.

Chodorow, N. (1971) 'Being and Doing: a Cross-Cultural Examination of the Socialization of Males and Females', in: V. Gornick and B. Moran (eds.), *Women in Sexist Society*. New York: Basic Books. pp. 259–291.

Chodorow, N. (1978) *The Reproduction of Mothering: Psychoanalysis and the Sociology of Gender*. Berkeley: University of California Press.

Chuchryk, P. (1984) 'Protest, Politics, and Personal Life: the Emergence of Feminism in a Military Dictatorship, Chile, 1973–1983'. Unpublished dissertation, York University, Toronto, Canada.

Cole, J. (1979) 'Fair Science: Women in the Scientific Community', *Women's Studies International Forum*, 5 (1): 75–81.

Cole, J.R. and Zuckerman, H. (1987) 'Marriage, Motherhood and Research Performance in Science', *Scientific American*, 256: 83–89.

Connell, R.W. (1987) *Gender and Power*. Cambridge: Polity Press.

Cooperstock, R. (1978) 'Sex Differences in Psychotropic Drug Use', *Social Science and Medicine*, 12B: 179–186.

Cott, N. (1986) 'Feminist Theory and Feminist Movements: the Past before Us', in: J. Mitchell and A. Oakley (eds.), *What Is Feminism? A Re-examination*. New York: Pantheon. pp. 49–63.

Coutinho-Wiggelendam, A. (1981) 'Vrouwenemancipatie rond de eeuwwisseling en het verzet daartegen', *Tijdschrift voor Vrouwenstudies*, 2 (2): 214–241.

Covarrubias, P. (1978) 'El movimiento feminista Chileno', in: P. Covarrubias and R. Franco (eds.), *Chile: mujer y sociedad*. Santiago: UNICEF. pp. 67–75.

Coward, R. (1983a) 'Is er een algemene theorie van vrouwelijkheid mogelijk? *Tijdschrift voor Vrouwenstudies*, 4: 529–544.

Coward, R. (1983b) *Patriarchal Precedents: Sexuality and Social Relations*. London: Routledge & Kegan Paul.

Crummet, M. de los Angeles (1977) 'El Poder Femenino: the Mobilization of Women against Socialism in Chile', *Latin American Perspectives*, 15 (4): 103–113.

Culpepper, E. (1978) 'Exploring Menstrual Attitudes', in: M.S. Hennifin (ed.), *Women Looking at Biology Looking at Women*. Cambridge, MA: Schenckman.

Davis, A. (1981) *Women, Race and Class*. Random House, New York.

Davis, Kathy (1986) 'The Process of Problem (Re)formulation in Psychotherapy', *Sociology of Health and Illness*, 8, (1): 44-74.

Davis, K. (1988a) 'Paternalism under the Microscope', in: A.D. Todd and S. Fisher (eds.), *Gender and Discourse: the Power of Talk*. Norwood: Ablex Publishing Company. pp. 19-54.

Davis, K. (1988b) *Power under the Microscope: Toward a Grounded Theory of Gender Relations in Medical Encounters*. Dordrecht: Foris Publications.

Dekkers, H. and Smeets, M. (1982) *Sekse-ongelijkheid op school: eigenschappen en leerprestaties van meisjes*. Nijmegen: Institute for Applied Sociology (ITS).

Delmar, R. (1986) 'What is Feminism?' in: J. Mitchell and A. Oakley (eds.), *What is Feminism? A Re-examination*. New York: Pantheon. pp. 8-34.

Derde nota onderwijsemancipatie (1983) *Een stukje wijzer*. Den Haag: Staatsuitgeverij.

Derriks, M. (1983) 'Studie-uitval van vrouwelijke studenten uit het wetenschappelijk onderwijs: een literatuurstudie', *Tijdschrift voor Vrouwenstudies*, 4 (1): 83-95.

Di Maggio, P. (1979) 'Review Essay: On Pierre Bourdieu', *American Journal of Sociology*, 84 (6): 1460-1474.

Doorne-Huiskes, A. van (1983) *Posities van vrouwen en mannen aan de Rijksuniversiteit Utrecht*. Utrecht: Vakgroep sociologie en socialisatie, University of Utrecht.

Doorne-Huiskes, A. van (1986) *Loopbanen van vrouwen en mannen: een analyse*. Utrecht: Vakgroep theoretische sociologie en methodenleer, University of Utrecht.

Dweck, C.S., Davidson, W., Nelson, S. and Enna, B. (1978) 'Sex Differences in Learned Helplessness', *Developmental Psychology*, 4 (3): 268-276.

van Eck, E. and Veeken, L. (1986) 'Wiskunde, niets voor meisjes?' *Pedagogische Studieën*, 63 (7/8): 293-303.

Ehrenreich, B. and English, D. (1979) *For Her Own Good*. London: Pluto Press.

Eisenstein, H. and Jardine, A. (eds.) (1987) *The Future of Difference*. New Brunswick: Rutgers University Press.

Eisenstein, Z.R. (ed.) (1979) *Capitalist Patriarchy and the Case for Socialist Feminism*. New York: Monthly Review Press.

Elias, N. (1972) *Wat is sociologie?* Utrecht: Het Spectrum.

184   THE GENDER OF POWER

Engels, F. (1884) *The Origin of the Family, Private Property and the State*. New York: International Publishers, 1972.

Etienne, M. and Leacock, E. (eds.) (1980) *Women and Colonization: Anthropological Perspectives*. New York: Praeger.

Fee, E. (1986) 'Critiques of Modern Science: the Relationship of Feminism to Other Radical Epistemologies', in: R. Bleier (ed.), *Feminist Approaches to Science*. New York: Pergamon Press. pp. 42–56.

Fidell, L.S. (1970) 'Empirical Verification of Sex Discrimination in Living: Practices in Psychology', *American Psychologist*, 25 (12): 1094–1097.

Fidell, L. S. (1980) 'Sex Role Stereotypes and the American Physician', *Psychology of Women Quarterly*, 4 (3): 313–330.

Firestone, S. (1971) *The Dialectic of Sex*. New York: Morrow.

Fisher, S. (1986) *In the Patient's Best Interest: Women and the Politics of Medical Decisions*. New Brunswick, NJ: Rutgers University Press.

Fisher, S. and Groce, S.B. (1985) 'Doctor–Patient Negotiation of Cultural Assumptions', *Sociology of Health and Illness*, 7 (3): 342–374.

Fisher, S. and Todd, A.D. (eds.) (1983) *The Social Organization of Doctor–Patient Communication*. Washington, DC: Center For Applied Linguistics.

Fisher, S. and Todd, A.D. (eds.) (1986) *Discourse and Institutional Authority: Medicine, Education and Law*. Norwood: Ablex Publishing Company.

Fishman, P.M. (1978) 'Interaction: the Work Women Do', *Social Problems*, 26: 397–406.

Fluer-Lobben, C. (1987) 'Marxism and the Matriarchate', *Critique of Anthropology*, 7 (1): 5–14.

Foucault, M. (1980) *Power/Knowledge: Selected Interviews and Other Writings, 1972–1977*, edited by C. Gordon. New York: Pantheon Books.

Foucault, M. (1983) 'Afterword: the Subject of Power', in: H. Dreyfus and P. Rabinow (eds.), *Michel Foucault: Beyond Structuralism and Hermeneutics*. Chicago: University of Chicago Press. pp. 208–226.

Franssen, A. and van Heezik, N. (1987) *Ongehuwd bestaan: ongehuwde vrouwen in de jaren vijftig*. Amsterdam: SUA.

Friedl, E. (1967) 'The Position of Women: Appearance and Reality', *Anthropological Quarterly*, 40: 97–108.

Garfinkel, H. (1967) *Studies in Ethnomethodology*. Englewood Cliffs, NJ: Prentice-Hall.

Garnham, N. and Williams, R. (1980) 'Pierre Bourdieu and the Sociology of Culture: an Introduction', *Media, Culture and Society*, 2 (3): 209–223.

Geertz, C. (1973) *The Interpretation of Cultures*. New York: Basic Books.

Gergen, K.J. (1980) 'Developments in Theory toward Intellectual Audacity in Social Psychology', in: R. Gilmour and S. Duck (eds.), *The Development of Social Psychology*. London: Academic Press. pp. 239–271.

Gergen, M.M. and Gergen, K.J. (1984) 'The Social Construction of Narrative Accounts', in: K.J. Gergen and M.M. Gergen (eds.), *Historical Social Psychology*. Hillsdale: Lawrence Erlbaum. pp. 173–191.

Gerson, J.M. and Peiss, K. (1985) 'Boundaries, Negotiation, Consciousness: Reconceptualizing Gender Relations', *Social Problems*, 32 (4): 317–331.

Giddens, A. (1976) *New Rules of Sociological Method*. London: Hutchinson.

Giddens, A. (1979) *Central Problems in Social Theory*. London: Macmillan Press.

Giddens, A. (1984) *The Constitution of Society*. Cambridge: Polity Press.

Godelier, M. (1986) *The Making of Great Men: Male Domination and Power among the New Guinea Baruya*. Cambridge: Cambridge University Press.

Goody, J. (1973) 'Bridewealth and Dowry in Africa and Eurasia', in: J. Goody and S. Tambiah, *Bridewealth and Dowry*. Cambridge: Cambridge University Press.

Goody, J. (1976) *Production and Reproduction*. Cambridge: Cambridge University Press.

Goody, J. (1990) *The Oriental, the Ancient and the Primitive: Systems of Marriage and the Family in the Pre-industrial Societies of Eurasia*. Cambridge: Cambridge University Press.

Goody, J. and Tambiah, S. (1973) *Bridewealth and Dowry*. Cambridge: Cambridge University Press.

Gramsci, A. (1971) *Selections from the Prison Notebooks*. London: Lawrence & Wishart.

Granqvist, H. (1931) *Marriage Conditions in a Palestinian Village*, vol. 1. Helsingfors: Akademische Buchhandlung.

Granqvist, H. (1935) *Marriage Conditions in a Palestinian Village*, vol. 2. Helsingfors: Akademische Buchhandlung.

Gremmen, C.C.M. and Westerbeek-van Eerten, J.A. (1988) *De kracht van de macht: theorieën over macht en hun gebruik in vrouwenstudies*. The Hague: STEO.

Grotenhuis, S. (1984) 'Opvoeden tot een gezonde omgang der geslachten: de diskussie over ko-edukatie in de jaren '50', *Tijdschrift voor Vrouwenstudies*, 19: 351–372.

Grunell, M. (1984) *Thuis in de jaren vijftig*. Amsterdam: Sociologisch Instituut, University of Amsterdam.

Grunell, M. (1986) 'Vanzelfsprekendheid: scharnier tussen zelfbepaling en lot', *Lover*, 86 (3): 162–169.

Hagemann-White, C. (1989) 'Geslacht en gedrag', in: S. Sevenhuijsen et al. (eds.), *Socialisties-Feministiese Teksten*, 11. Baarn: Ambo. pp. 33–48.

Haley, J. (1969) *The Power Tactics of Jesus Christ*. New York: Avon.

Harding, S. (1986) *The Science Question in Feminism*. Ithaca and London: Cornell University Press.

Harding, S. and Hintikka, M. (1983) *Discovering Reality: Feminist Perspectives on Epistemology, Metaphysics, Methodology and Philosophy of Science*. Dordrecht: D. Reidel.

Harris, O. and Young, K. (1981) 'Engendered Structures: Some Problems in the Analysis of Reproduction', in: J. Llobera and J. Kahn (eds.), *Anthropological Analysis and Pre-Capitalist Societies*. London: Macmillan.

Hartmann, H. (1979a) 'Capitalism, Patriarchy, and Job Segregation by Sex', in: Z. Eisenstein (ed.), *Capitalist Patriarchy and the Case for Socialist Feminism*. New York: Monthly Review Press. pp. 206–247.

Hartmann, H. (1979b) 'The Unhappy Marriage between Marxism and Feminism', *Capital and Class*, 3: 1–33.

Hartsock, N. (1983) *Money, Sex and Power: Toward a Feminist Historical Materialism*. New York: Longman.

Hartsock, N. (1987) 'Foucault on Power: a Theory for Women?' in: M. Leijenaar et al. (eds.), *The Gender of Power: A Symposium*. Leiden: Vakgroep Vrouwenstudies.

Hawkins, A.C. and Balen, B. van (1984) 'De positie van vrouwen in het wetenschappelijk onderwijs van 1970-1980', *Universiteit & Hogeschool*, 30 (4): 194-209.

Hayley, F.A. (1923) *A Treatise on the Laws and Customs of the Sinhalese, Including Portions Still Surviving under the Name of Kandyan Law*. Colombo: Cave and Co.

Henley, N.M. (1977) *Body Politics: Power, Sex and Nonverbal Communication*. Englewood Cliffs, NJ: Prentice Hall.

Hirshon, R. (ed.) (1984) *Women and Property, Women as Property*. New York: St Martin's Press.

Homans, H. (ed.) (1985) *The Sexual Politics of Reproduction*. Aldershot: Gower.

de Jager, H. and Mok, A.L. (1971) *Grondbeginselen der sociologie*. Leiden: Stenfert Kroese.

Johnson, P. (1978) 'Women and Interpersonal Power', in: I. Frieze et al. (eds.), *Women and Sex Roles*. New York: Norton.

Joppke, C. (1987), 'The Cultural Dimensions of Class Formation and Class Struggle in the Social Theory of Pierre Bourdieu', *Berkeley Journal of Sociology*, 31: 53-78.

Jungbluth, P. and Schotel-Kraetzer, S. (1982) *Sekseongelijkheid op school: onderwijsinrichting en onderwijsbeleid*. Nijmegen: Institute of Applied Sociology (ITS).

Kanter, R.M. (1977a) *Men and Women of the Corporation*. New York: Basic Books.

Kanter, R.M. (1977b) 'Some Effects of Proportions on Group Life', *American Journal of Sociology*, 82: 965-990.

Kien, J. and Cassidy, D. (1984) 'The History of Women in Science: a Seminar at the University of Regensburg, FRG', *Women's Studies International Forum*, 7 (4): 313-318.

Kipnis, D. (1976) *The Power Holders*. Chicago: The University of Chicago Press.

Kirkwood, J. (1990) *Ser política en Chile: los nudos de la sabiduría feminista*. Santiago de Chile: Editorial Cuarto Propio.

Klaver, I. and Onstenk, J. (1985) 'De jacht op het dagelijks leven', *Krisis* 21: 41-59.

Knijn, T. (1985) 'Moederschap in Nederland: geleefde beelden', *LOVA-Nieuwsbrief*, 6 (3): 87-90.

Knox, R. (1911) *An Historical Relation of Ceylon*. London: Chiswell.

Koenders, A. and Wolffensperger, J. (1986) *Vrouwelijk wetenschappelijke personeel aan de LH*. Wageningen: Vakgroep Vrouwenstudies.

Komter, A.E. (1979) *Macht in relatie tussen vrouwen en mannen.* Nijmegen: Vakgroep Sociale Psychologie, Katholieke Universiteit Nijmegen.

Komter, A.E. (1985) *De macht van de vanzelfsprekendheid.* Den Haag: VUGA.

Komter, A.E. (1988) 'De constructie van dilemma's in het feminisme', *Tijdschrift voor Vrouwenstudies*, 2: 176–93.

Komter, A.E. (1989a) 'Hidden Power in Marriage', *Gender and Society*, 2: 187–216.

Komter, A.E. (1989b) 'Macht, verantwoordelijkheid en de verhouding tussen de seksen', in: M. Bovens et al. (eds.), *Verantwoordelijkheid: retoriek en realiteit.* Zwolle: Tjeenk Willink. pp. 141–160.

Lamphere, L. (1977) 'Anthropology', *Signs*, 2 (3): 612–627.

de Lauretis, T. (1987) *Technologies of Gender: Essays on Theory, Film and Fiction.* Bloomington: Indiana University Press.

Leacock, E. (1981) *Myths of Male Dominance: Collected Articles on Women Cross-Culturally.* New York: Monthly Review Press.

Lechner, N. and Levy, L. (1984) *Notas sobre la vida cotidiana III: el disciplinamiento de la mujer.* Material de Discusión no. 57. Santiago de Chile: FLACSO.

Lenanne, K.J. and Lenanne, J. (1973) 'Alleged Psychogenic Disorders in Women – a Possible Manifestation of Sexual Prejudice', *New England Journal of Medicine*, 288 (6): 288–292.

Lewis, J. (ed.) (1983) *Women's Welfare and Women's Rights.* London and Canberra: Croom Helm.

Lorber, J. (1976) 'Women and Medical Sociology: Invisible Professionals and Ubiquitous Patients', in: M. Millman and R. Moss Kanter (eds.), *In Another Voice: Feminist Perspectives on Social Life and Social Science.* New York: Octagon Books.

Lukes, S. (1974) *Power: a Radical View.* London: Macmillan.

Lukes, S. (1979) 'On the Relativity of Power', in: S.C. Brown (ed.), *Philosophical Disputes in the Social Sciences.* Sussex: Harvester Press, Ltd. pp. 261–274.

Lukes, S. (1982) 'Panoptikon: Macht und Herrschaft bei Weber, Marx, Foucault', *Kursbuch*, 70: 135–148.

Lukes, S. (1986) *Power.* Oxford: Blackwell.

MacCormack, C. (1980) 'Nature, Culture and Gender: a Critique', in C. MacCormack and M. Strathern (eds.), *Nature, Culture and Gender.* Cambridge: Cambridge University Press.

MacPherson, A. (ed.) (1988) *Women's Problems in General Practice*. Oxford: Oxford University Press.

MacPherson, C.B. (1962) *The Political Theory of Possessive Individualism*. Oxford: Oxford University Press.

Maguire, P. (1984) *Women in Development: an Alternative Analysis*. Amherst: Center for International Education, University of Massachusetts.

Maher, V. (1974) *Women and Property in Morocco*. Cambridge: Cambridge University Press.

Martin, B.R. and Irvine, J. (1982) 'Women in Science: the Astronomical Brain Drain', *Women's Studies International Forum*, 7 (4): 313–318.

Martin, E. (1987) *The Woman in the Body: a Cultural Analysis of Reproduction*. Boston: Beacon Press.

Mattelart, M. (1975) 'Chile: the Feminine Side of the Coup or When Bourgeois Women Take to the Streets', *NACLA's Latin America Empire Report*, 9: 14–25.

McDonald, G.W. (1980) 'Family Power: a Decade of Theory and Research, 1970–1979', *Journal of Marriage and the Family*, 29: 345–52.

McKechnie, J.L. (ed.) (1971) *Webster's New 20th Century Dictionary of the English Language*. Cleveland/New York: World Publishing Company.

Medina, C. (1985) 'Women's Rights as Human Rights: Latin American Countries and the Organization of American States (OAS)', in: M. Díaz-Diocarets and I.M. Zavala (eds.), *Women, Feminist Identity and Society in the 1980s: Selected Papers*. Amsterdam and Philadelphia: John Benjamin. pp. 63–79.

Meehan, E.M. (1985) *Women's Right at Work: Campaigns and Policy in Britain and the United States*. London: Macmillan.

Meyer, J.L. (1983) 'Sekse als organisatieprincipe'. Unpublished dissertation, Amsterdam: Vakgroep SAOP, Universiteit van Amsterdam.

Meyer, J.L. (forthcoming) *Preferences of Parents-to-be and the Interpretation of Behaviour of New Born Infants*. The Hague: Ministry of Social Affairs and Job Opportunities.

Meza, M.A. (ed.) (1985) *La otra mitad de Chile*. Santiago de Chile: INC, CESOC, Ediciones Chile y América.

Mies, M. and Reddock, R. (eds.) (1982) *National Liberation and Women's Liberation*. The Hague: Institute of Social Studies.

Millett, K. (1969) *Sexual Politics*. London: Abacus.

Mitchell, J. (1971) *Woman's Estate*. Harmondsworth: Penguin Books.

Mitchell, J. (1974) *Psychoanalysis and Feminism*. London: Allan Lane.

Mitchell, J. and Oakley, A. (eds.) (1986) *What is Feminism? A Re-examination*. New York: Pantheon Books.

Mitchell, J. and Rose, J. (1982) *Feminine Sexuality, Jacques Lacan and the Ecole Freudienne*. London: Macmillan.

Moors, A. (1990) 'Gender Hierarchy in a Palestinian Village: the Case of Al-Balad', in: K. Glavanis and P. Glavanis (eds.), *The Rural Middle East: Peasant Lives and Modes of Production*. London: Zed Press. pp. 195–210.

Moore, H. (1988) *Feminism and Anthropology*. Cambridge: Polity Press.

Moscovici, S. (1976) *Social Influence and Social Change*. London: Academic Press.

Moscovici, S. (1985) 'Social Influence and Conformity', in: G. Lindzey and E. Aronson (eds.), *The Handbook of Social Psychology*. New York: Random House. pp. 347–413.

Moscovici, S. and Faucheux, C. (1972) 'Social Influence, Conformity Bias and the Study of Active Minorities', in: L. Berkowitz (ed.), *Advances in Experimental Social Psychology 6*. New York: Academic Press. pp. 149–202.

Mulder, M. (1972) *Het spel om de macht*. Wolvega: Taconis.

Munters, Q.J., Meijer E., Mommaas, H., Poel, H. v.d., Rosendal, R. and G. Spaargaren (1985) *Anthony Giddens: een kennismaking met de structuratietheorie*. Wageningen: Landbouwhogeschool Wageningen.

Nandy, A. (1983) *The Intimate Enemy: Loss and Recovery of Self under Colonialism*. Delhi: Oxford University Press.

Nelson, C. (1974) 'Public and Private Politics: Women in the Middle Eastern World', *American Ethnologist*, 1: 551–563.

Oakley, A. (1972) *Sex, Gender and Society*. New York: Harper Colophon Books.

Oakley, A. (1979) 'A Case of Maternity: Paradigms of Women as Maternity Cases', *Signs*, 4 (4): 607–631.

Obeyesekera, G. (1967) *Land Tenure in Village Ceylon: a Sociological and Historical Study*. Cambridge: Cambridge University Press.

O'Brien, M. (1981) *The Politics of Reproduction*. Boston: Routledge & Kegan Paul.

Ortner, S. and Whitehead, H. (eds.) (1981) *Sexual Meanings: the Cultural Construction of Gender and Sexuality.* Cambridge: Cambridge University Press.

Ott, M. (1985) *Assepoesters en kroonprinsen.* Amsterdam: SUA.

Oudijk, C. (1983) *Sociale atlas van de vrouw.* The Hague: Staatsuitgeverij.

Outshoorn, J. (1981) 'Feminisme en marxisme: het relaas van een echtscheiding op zoek naar een omgangsregeling', *Tijdschrift voor Vrouwenstudies,* 3: 339-360.

Outshoorn, J. (1986) *De politieke strijd rondom de abortuswetgeving in Nederland 1964-1984.* Amsterdam: VUGA.

Outshoorn J. (1989) *Een irriterend onderwerp: verschuivende conceptualiseringen van het sekseverschil.* Nijmegen: SUN.

Parsons, T. (1963) 'On the Concept of Political Power', *Proceedings of the American Philosophical Society,* 107: 232-262.

Peebles, P. (1973) The Transformation of a Colonial Elite: The Mudaliyars of 19th century Ceylon. University of Chicago, Ph.D. thesis.

Peiris, P.E. (1909) *Ribeiro's History of Ceilao.* Colombo: De Conto.

Peiris, R. (1956) *Sinhalese Social Organization.* Colombo: Ceylon University Press.

Pels, D. (1986) *Property or Power? A Study in Intellectual Rivalry.* Amsterdam: University of Amsterdam.

Reskin, B.F. (1978) 'Scientific Productivity, Sex and Location in the Institution of Science', *American Journal of Sociology,* 83 (5): 1235-1243.

Riley, D. (1988) '*Am I that Name?' Feminism and the Category of 'Women' in History.* London: Macmillan.

Risseeuw, C. (1986) *Changing Inheritance Rights of Sinhalese Women under Colonial Rule.* The Hague: WOTRO Yearbook.

Risseeuw, C. (1988) *The Fish don't Talk about Water: Gender Transformation, Power, and Resistance among Women in Sri Lanka.* Leiden: E.J. Brill. (Republished by Manohar, Delhi, 1991.)

Roberts, M. (1975a) *Facts of Modern Ceylon History through the Letters of Jeronis Peiris.* Colombo: Hansa Publishers.

Roberts, M. (1975b) 'Some Aspects of Economic and Social Policy in Ceylon, 1840-1871'. PhD thesis, University of Oxford.

Römkens, R. (1980) *Vrouwenmishandeling: een studie over geweld, macht, verzet.* Nijmegen: Katholieke Universiteit Nijmegen.

Rosaldo, M.Z. and Lamphere, L. (eds.) (1974) *Women, Culture and Society.* Stanford: Stanford University Press.

Rosenfeld, H. (1980) 'Men and Women in Arab Peasant to Proletariat Transformation', in: S. Diamond (ed.), *Theory and Practice: Essays Presented to Gene Weltfish*. The Hague: Mouton. pp. 195–219.

Ross, E. and Rapp, R. (1981) 'Sex and Society: a Research Note from History and Anthropology', *Comparative Studies in Society and History*, 23: 51–73.

Rowbotham, S. (1972) *Women, Resistance and Revolution: a History of Women and Revolution in the Modern World*. New York: Vintage Books.

Rubin, G. (1975) 'The Traffic in Women: Notes on the "Political Economy" of Sex', in: R. Reiter (ed.), *Towards an Anthropology of Women*. New York: Monthly Review Press. pp. 57–210.

Rubin, L. (1985) *Intieme vreemden: hoe mensen in relaties met elkaar omgaan*. Baarn: Ambo.

Sacks, H., Schegloff, E.A. and Jefferson, G. (1974) 'A Simple Systematics for the Organization of Turn-taking in Conversation', *Language*, 50: 696–735.

Saharso, S. and Westerbeek, J. (1983) *De precaire balans: een reconstructie van ervaringen van vrouwelijke studenten met studeren, achterraken en uitvallen*. Amsterdam: Universiteit van Amsterdam.

Sarkar, N.K. (1957) *The Demography of Ceylon*. Ceylon: Government Press Ceylon.

Sayers, J., Evans, M. and Redclift, N. (eds.) (1987) *Engels Revisited: New Feminist Essays*. London: Tavistock.

Schuyt, C.J.M. (1973) *Rechtvaardigheid en effectiviteit in de verdeling van levenskansen*. Rotterdam: Rotterdamse Universitaire Press.

Schwarzer, A. (1974) *Het kleine verschil en de grote gevolgen*. Baarn: Ambo.

Scott, J. (1986) 'Gender: a Useful Category of Historical Analysis', *American Historical Review*, 91: 1053–1075.

Scott, J. (1988) 'Deconstructing Equality-versus-Difference: or, The Uses of Poststructuralist Theory for Feminism', *Feminist Studies*, 14: 33–65.

Scully, D. (1980) *Men Who Control Women's Health*. Boston: Houghton Mifflin.

Scully, D. and Bart, P. (1973) 'A Funny Thing Happened on the Way to the Orifice: Women in Gynecological Textbooks', *American Journal of Sociology*, 78: 1045–1050.

Segal, L. (1987) *Is the Future Female? Troubled Thoughts on Contemporary Feminism*. London: Virago.

Sen, G. and Grown, C. (1985) *Dawn: Development Alternatives with Women for a New Era*. Norway: Verbum.

Smith, D.E. (1979) 'A Sociology for Women', in: J.A. Sherman and E. Torton Beck (eds.), *The Prism of Sex: Essays in the Sociology of Knowledge*. Madison: University of Wisconsin Press. pp. 302–331.

Snodgrass, D.R. (1966) *Ceylon, an Export Economy in Transition*. Homewood, IL: Irwin.

Sommer, A. (1985) 'Het verschil en de gelijkheid: inleiding bij de lezingen', *Tijdschrift voor Vrouwenstudies*, 4: 382–395.

Standing, H. (1980) 'Sickness is a Woman's Business? Reflections on the Attribution of Illness', in: Brighton Women and Science Group (eds.), *Alice through the Microscope*. London: Virago.

Stanley, L. and Wise, S. (1983) *Breaking Out: Feminist Consciousness and Feminist Research*. London: Routledge & Kegan Paul.

Stevens, E. (1973) 'Marianismo: the Other Face of Machismo in Latin America', in: R. Pescatello (ed.), *Female and Male in Latin America: Essays*. Pittsburgh: University of Pittsburgh Press. pp. 90–101.

Stolte-Heiskanen, V. (1983) 'The Role and Status of Women Scientific Workers in Research Groups', *Research in the Interweave of Social Roles*, 3: 59–87.

Sullerot, E. (1969) *Vrouwenarbeid in onze tijd*. Bussum: Paul Brand.

Swartz, D. (1977) 'Pierre Bourdieu: The Cultural Transmission of Social Inequality', *Harvard Educational Review*, 47 (4): 545–555.

Tambiah, S. (1973) 'Dowry and Bridewealth and the Property Rights of Women in South Asia', in: J. Goody and S. Tambiah (eds.), *Bridewealth and Dowry*. Cambridge: Cambridge University Press.

Tambiah, S. (1989) 'Bridewealth and Dowry Revisited: the Position of Women in Sub-Saharan Africa and North India', *Current Anthropology*, 30 (4): 413–435.

Tennekes, J. (1987) 'Religie, cultuur en macht', in: J.W. Bakker et al. (eds.), *Antropologie tussen wetenschap en kunst. Essays over Clifford Geertz*. Amsterdam: VU Uitgeverij.

Thompson, J.B. (1984) *Studies in the Theory of Ideology*. Cambridge: Polity Press.

Tricht, A. van (1957) *De toekomst tegemoet. Beroepsmogelijkheden voor meisjes*. Haarlem: De Spaarnestad.

Trömel-Plötz, S. (1984) *Gewalt durch Sprache*. Frankfurt am Main: Fischer Taschenbuch Verlag.

den Uyl, M. (1986) 'Matrilineariteit, vrouwenruil en Oedipale crissis: een commentaar op Gayle Rubin: "De handel in vrouwen"', *Antropologische Verkenningen*, 5 (4): 21–41.

Veeken, L. (1982) *Kiezen en delen: faktoren in het onderwijs die van invloed zijn op de onderwijskeuzen van meisjes*. Amsterdam: SCO.

Veerman, H. and Verheijen, C. (1984) *Beroepsarbeid en gezin: vrouwen in een spanningsveld?* Deventer: Van Loghum Slaterus.

Verheijen, C. (1986) 'Moederschap: gecontroleerde zelfbeschikking', *Jeugd en samenleving*, 16 (3/4): 131–139.

Verwayen-Leijh, R.M. (1985) *Studieuitval en vertraging van vrouwen in het hoger onderwijs*. 's Gravenhage: Studiecentrum OTO.

de Vries, P. (1987) '"Het persoonlijke is politiek" en het ontstaan van de tweede golf in Nederland 1968–1973', in: S. Sevenhuijsen et al. (eds.), *Socialisties-Feministiese Teksten*, 10. Baarn: Ambo. pp. 15–35.

Waithe, M.E. (ed.) (1987) *A History of Women Philosophers: Ancient Women Philosophers, 600 BC – AD 500*, vol. 1. Dordrecht: Nijhoff.

Walker, A. (1984) *In Search of our Mothers' Gardens*. London: The Women's Press.

Watzlawick, P., Beavin, J.H. and Jackson, D.D. (1967) *Pragmatics of Human Communication*. New York: Norton & Co.

Weber, M. (1978) *Economy and Society*, Guenther Roth and Claus Wittich (eds. and trans.) Berkeley and Los Angeles: University of California Press.

Weiss, R.S. (1975) *Marital Separation*. New York: Basic Books.

Wertheim, W.F. (1964) *East–West Parallels: Sociological Approaches to Modern Asia*. The Hague: Van Hoeve.

Whitehead, A. (1984) 'Men and Women, Kinship and Property: Some General Issues', in: R. Hirshon (ed.), *Women and Property, Women as Property*. New York: St Martin's Press. pp. 176–191.

Wilson, E. (1986) *Hidden Agendas*. London: Tavistock Publications.

Wolffensperger, J. (1987) 'Feminist Education within a University Setting: on Unacknowledged Conditions and Unintended Consequences of Women's Studies'. Paper for the Third International Interdisciplinary Congress on Women, Dublin, Ireland.

Zinn, H. (1980) *A People's History of the United States*. New York: Harper Colophon Books.

Index